VICTORIA ANDER

CW00688119

★ ★ ★

THE ESSENTIAL UK

AIR FRYER

COOKBOOK

Quick, Easy, Delicious & Nutritious Air Fried Recipes Including Dinners, Lunches & Breakfasts Using UK Measurements & Ingredients

★ ★ ★

Table of Contents

Introduction

The familiar, crispy crunch, moist, and chewy middle of fried chicken or French fries greet you with joy as soon as you bite into them. However, the delicious flavour of fried dishes has a price. Doctors have proven that the cooking oils used to prepare them can lead to conditions like cancer, type 2 diabetes, and heart disease.

What should be done to avoid these issues while also savouring the yummy and crispy texture of fried foods?

Air fryers are a new gadget on the market that will look amazing on any countertop. They are a kitchen gadget that claims to replicate the flavour, texture, and golden-brown colour of foods that are fried in oil without the excess fat and calories. But do these alternatives to deep fryers live up to their claims?

The air fryer somewhat fries your food, functioning more like an upgraded convection oven. The small device makes the bold claim that it can deep-fry food using just hot air and little-to-no oil. You can fry a variety of foods, including fresh baked cookies, roasted veggies, homemade French fries, and frozen chicken wings in an air fryer.

Air fryers are mostly around the size of a coffee machine, making them great for countertops. You load up a slide-out basket with the items you want to fry, such as diced potatoes, chicken nuggets, and courgette slices. You can treat it lightly with oil if you'd like and cook up to 200°C. Then, hot air is circulated around the food by a blower. Hence, working like a convection oven but better.

Similar to deep-fried dishes, the spinning air cooks the exterior of food first, giving it a golden crispy coating while keeping the inside soft. Any grease that drips as the food cooks is caught in a container that is below the basket. Without using much oil, air fryers produce great crunchy, chewy delicacies that people enjoy.

Nearly all kitchens are tight on counter space. However, you should create space for an air fryer as it is becoming a necessity. They are the newest trend in home kitchens and are now prominently used for thousands of recipes.

Here is what you need to know to quickly start air frying.

The Cooking Process in an Air Fryer

A heating system and fan are located in the top portion of an air fryer. When the air fryer is turned on, hot air is blown over and around the food placed in the basket. This quick circulation gives the meal a crisp texture similar to deep-frying without the need of much oil. Hot air is circulated quickly by a fan, which uses a browning process called the Maillard reaction to create a crisp coating.

The Maillard reaction is a process where food changes colour and acquires flavour through browning. It happens by a chemical reaction between amino acids and reducing sugars to create a browning and crisping effect around foods. Typically, Maillard reactions only start to happen above 140°C and may require higher heat for better crisping. It is an instance of non-enzymatic browning, similar to caramelization.

Regular frying techniques, however, dip food in heated oil that is mostly higher than the boiling point of water, to effect the Maillard reaction at temperatures between 140°C and 165°C.

While the air fryer may allow heat heights of up to 200°C, most of them allow for temperature and timer adjustments to control exact cooking and browning.

Differences Between the Air Fryer and the Oven

An air fryer is similar to an oven in that it bakes and roasts food, but it differs from an oven in that it uses less oil than a conventional oven and has heating elements that are only on top. This makes food incredibly crispy in a matter of minutes. Due to the focused heat source and the location and size of the fan, they heat up fast and cook food quicker and more evenly than an oven.

The clean-up is just another fantastic benefit of air frying. Most air fryer racks and baskets can go in the dishwasher unlike for an oven. For those that can't, I advise using a decent dish brush to clean them.

Types of Air Fryers

There are many different kinds of air fryers and air fryer-related products available. When choosing, following this guide will help you make the perfect choice:

BASKET AIR FRYER

This air fryer is the most known type. They come in a variety of shapes that contain a removable basket for loading and cooking food within.

Because the basket has holes all around it, hot air from the appliance's top can flow around the food with ease and for even cooking. The basket typically has a handle, also making it simpler for handling and tossing foods.

PADDLE AIR FRYER

Paddle air fryers have a removable basket, so they have a similar appearance to basket air fryers. However, paddle versions also have a feature that normal basket models do not: it self-stirs.

These paddle variants have a spinning, detachable paddle in the middle of the basket. Your time and effort will be saved because you won't need to pull the basket in and out of the oven while the food cooks, yet still achieve even cooking.

OVEN AIR FRYER

Oven air fryers are a popular subcategory. They function similarly to the aforementioned varieties by circulating your meal with hot air that comes from the top. But their shapes are what really sets them apart from one another.

With their square or rectangular dimensions, oven air fryers resemble toaster ovens rather closely. Baking trays and racks are also included.

The best part about them is that you can bake, broil, roast, or dehydrate your meals with these products.

HALOGEN AIR FRYER

This kind is renowned for its glass construction, which allows you to better monitor your cooking. It might operate a little differently, although heat is also generated and circulated around the food using the halogen light.

Additionally, the device's heating mechanism is located on the top. This type is not intended to shake the food; you must flip it manually. The good news is that halogen air fryers are often large and can accommodate more food like an entire turkey.

MICROWAVE AIR FRYER

This kind of microwave and air fryer combo is a great example because it comes in many highly regarded models. In essence, they resemble a standard microwave but with an additional air frying feature.

In a microwave air fryer, you can steam, roast, and broil your meals with minimal oil. In short, there is no better option than these items if you require a combination of microwaves and air fryers.

PRESSURE COOKER AIR FRYER

If you require a combination of a pressure cooker and an air fryer, this type is your best choice. Although dishes made in a pressure cooker rarely turn out crispy, if you want to give these goodies a crunchy, golden appearance, this air fryer feature will completely please you.

Some versions have a tonne of capabilities, including the ability to bake, roast, slow cook, air fry, and more. They are therefore more expensive than other types of simple air fryers.

Tips for Using an Air Fryer

Having heard the good word about the air fryer's ability to brown and crisp foods to the best golden colour, I believe you're in for all the tips to achieve this result. Here, I share useful air fryer advice to aid every recipe you make turn out wonderful.

DO NOT OVERCROWD THE BASKET.

The basket may tempt you to pack it up with so much food, so you can cook everything in one go. But trust me, your food won't turn out golden and crispy if you do so.

Excess food in the basket results in uneven cooking and may create steam between the foods that may just not crisp them. The trick to success, cook in batches.

ADD A LITTLE OIL TO YOUR FOOD IN THE BASKET.

Yes, the air fryer boasts of not requiring oil when cooking certain foods like fruits. But for the most parts, misting or tossing the food in the basket with a little oil, about a teaspoon would aid perfect browning and crisping.

USE FOIL FOR EASIER CLEAN-UP.

As exact as it sounds, to ease up the cleaning process, you can line the air fryer basket with foil. It catches little food drippings and oil while cooking, so you don't have to deal with them after your sumptuous meal. Simply, remove the foil when done cooking and discard it.

ESTABLISH THE TIME AND CLIMATE.

Unlike deep frying, you can set the time and temperature for which your food should cook at. This allows for even cooking and the perfect result that you desire. Following the recipe in question or the manual's cooking guide, you can adjust both timing and temperature for the perfect cook.

ALLOW FOOD TO COOK.

It is best to leave your food to cook until it is time to flip or stir it. That way, you give room for excellent cooking.

What Can You Cook in the Air Fryer?

A large variety of food, really. Roast vegetables, bake cookies, of course fry chicken, chips, battered fish, and even dehydrate fruits with it.

As the air fryer gets more advanced in function and discovery, I find that many more foods can be cooked with it. For safety, follow a trusted recipe and always keep the manual in close reach for verification.

Some options for first-hand tries are:

• FROZEN APPETISERS

The air fryer is a shining star for frozen foods. Think frozen French fries, frozen mozzarella sticks, chicken nuggets, and certain frozen vegetables. It cooks through the ice conveniently while drying out excess liquid for crispy results.

• HOMEMADE APPETISERS, SNACKS, AND SIDES

You get a terrific outcome with small foods with the air fryer. I particularly enjoy making breaded ravioli with it and that goes well for sweet potato fries, garlic fries, crusted pickles, and Parmesan chips too.

• MEAT, POULTRY, AND SEAFOOD

All meats, poultry, and seafood can be cooked in the air fryer. With a trusted recipe, dinners and lunches become such a breeze with the air fryer.

An interesting fact is that the air fryer may cook this category of foods in a shorter time than the oven. So, that's a speedy win for you.

• ROASTED VEGETABLES

Roasted vegetables are some of the best side dishes you can make with the air fryer. The air fryer's small space may mostly make vegetables for 2 to 4 servings; hence, for larger servings or for an occasion, you may need to create time for multiple batch cooking.

However, vegetables cook to perfection with the air fryer.

• **CERTAIN BAKED GOODS**

Single-serving desserts, including little baked goods like cookies, doughnut holes, and apple fritters, can be made in air fryers. Cakes can also be baked in it using an air fryer safe cake pan or dishes.

When considering baking desserts with runny batter directly in the basket, freeze them first to prevent mess or from damaging the air fryer.

Below, I assembled a food type, time, and temperature guide to help you use the air fryer at a standard level.

INGREDIENT	TEMP.	TIME	PREP GUIDE
Chicken breasts (170g each)	190°C	10 to 15 minutes	Brush with oil and seasoning and flip halfway through cooking.
Chicken wings (split, 450g)	200°C	20 to 25 minutes	Toss with oil and seasoning. Flip halfway through cooking.
Chicken thighs (bone-in)	200°C	20 to 25 minutes	Season and coat with little oil before cooking. Flip halfway through cooking.
Pork chops bone-in (3 cm thick)	200°C	10 to 15 minutes	Season and flip halfway through cooking.
Steak (3 cm thick)	200°C	10 to 15 minutes	Oil, season, and flip halfway through cooking.
Fish fillets 3 cm thick, 170 g each)	200°C	8 to 10 minutes	Brush with oil and season. No flipping required.
Sweet potatoes (cut into 3 cm wedges)	200°C	12 to 15 minutes	Toss with oil, season, and shake basket halfway through cooking.
Brussels sprouts, halved	200°C	10 to 15 minutes	Toss with oil, season, and shake basket twice through cooking.
Butternut squash	200°C	12 to 15 minutes	Toss with oil, season, and shake the basket halfway through cooking.
Frozen fries (450 g)	200°C	15 to 20 minutes	Shake twice while cooking.

Different Ways of Air Frying

Food that is air-fried has a similar flavour and texture to food that has been deep-fried: Juicy on the inside and crisp on the outside. However, depending on what you're cooking, you may only need to use a very small amount of oil, if any at all.

Therefore, if you use only 1-2 teaspoons of vegetable oil with seasoning and adhere to air frying vegetables than other foods, air frying is undoubtedly a healthier alternative to deep frying. The secret to managing weight, lowering the risk of chronic disease, and improving long-term health as our aim is to raise your family's veggie intake. In most cases, air frying is healthier than deep frying. It has much less fat and cuts back calories by 70-80%.

This cooking style may help limit other negative health impacts of oil frying. When you cook starchy foods, like potatoes, a reaction takes place that creates a chemical called acrylamide, which studies have linked to an increased risk of developing cancer. According to experts, air frying reduces acrylamide by 90% in fried potatoes.

However, not all aspects of air frying may be healthier for you. Air-frying fish increases the concentration of "cholesterol oxidation products" (COPs). When meat or fish is cooked, the cholesterol in such foods degrades, creating COPs. These compounds are linked to cancer, artery stiffening, coronary heart disease, and other illnesses. Adding fresh parsley, chives, or a combination of the two is one approach to reduce the quantity of COPs produced when air-frying fish. Herbs function as antioxidants to limit the COPs in foods made in the air fryer. As well, air frying reduces fish's omega-3 fatty acids. These "good fats" are great for heart health by reducing blood pressure, protecting the heart, and increasing levels of "good" HDL cholesterol.

How Do Foods Fried in the Air Fryer Taste?

Is air frying as tasty as conventional frying? In the end, it's a matter of opinion.

When you fry food, the batter soaks up the cooking oil. This keeps the centre of fried meals moist while giving the outside a pleasant crunch. Foods that have been fried also have a beautiful, deep colour to them. Air frying still creates a crisp, but won't offer the same appearance or mouthfeel as oil frying.

Some experts often compare oil and air frying and they observed that the two techniques produced meals with varied textures and sensory qualities but identical colour and moisture content.

Your cooking style also counts. Your food may cook unevenly, giving you some crunchy and some mushy patches, if you overcrowd the little basket.

Our Best Tips for Air Fryers

- Always preheat your air fryer for good heat circulation before introducing the food.
- Cooking in air fryers is quicker. Make sure to reduce the time (and temperature) at which you cook your meal if a recipe asks for a conventional oven!
- Air fryers may be rather noisy. If you discover that yours is noisy, don't worry!
- Unless otherwise specified in the recipe, always cook your meal in one layer. Like many other methods of cooking, air frying requires space to function properly. Give your basket plenty of room so that air can freely circulate around the food. Your meal will cook more slowly and get less crispy if it is crowded.
- Never load an air fryer with more than half of its capacity. Your food may not cook evenly and may be partially burned or uncooked.
- Use a little oil to get the deep-fried flavour you're after.
- To help prevent breaded things from adhering to the basket, dab some oil on a paper towel and wipe it over the contents. Aerosol sprays shouldn't be used directly on the baskets because they may eventually cause the non-stick coating to peel off. Instead, spray the food directly before it is placed in the air fryer.
- For a crispier and tastier result, reheat leftovers in your air fryer instead of the microwave. Face it, leftovers frequently lose their life and crispy textures in the microwave. Much faster than the oven, the air fryer will revive leftover pizza or roast veggies.
- Instead of just emptying the basket into a basin, remove food from your air fryer using silicone tongs. Do this to prevent scratching and to avoid any extra oil that can burn you or make your food soggy.
- Recognize that your air fryer's outside is hot (especially the back). Please don't touch it!
- Cutting food too thinly can cause it to burn easily or cause it to fly around and become caught in the air fryer due to the extreme heat and air that an air fryer employs. Keep your bite-sized cuts standard.
- Make sure meals that are battered are as dry as possible before placing them in the air fryer. You can also freeze them before air frying.
- Batter will probably dribble off before it cooks on many fried foods since they have a moist coating that won't cook properly in air fryers. When using an air fryer, it's better to use breadcrumbs. A desiccated surface allows the food to stay warm in the hot air storm without turning into "sawdust".
- It is advised to cook bacon at a temperature lower than the smoke point of bacon oil in order to prevent smoking or burning. For air frying bacon, I use 175°C for 5-7 minutes.
- The smoke point of the cooking oils you use is something to be aware of. Avoiding oils with low smoke points and cooking meals at lower temperatures is advised. You shouldn't burn, smoke, or spray oil on the heating element.
- Keep the heated basket away from your hands and the counters after using the air fryer. I usually set the hot air fryer basket down on a pot holder, silicone trivet, or hot pad after removing it from the appliance.

Cleaning an Air Fryer

Never forget to clean your air fryer, just like you would any other kitchen item. After each use, air fryers should at the very least be lightly cleaned, particularly the drawer and basket. Every few weeks, give your air fryer a thorough cleaning.

When cleaning your air fryer, avoid using any abrasive items or scrubbers and make sure the appliance is unplugged. While some air fryers have baskets and drawers that can be cleaned in the dishwasher, others require manual cleaning. Also, before placing any attachments in the dishwasher, consult your user manual!

Using the following air fryer accessories can make clean-up even simpler:

1. Silicone liner
2. Parchment paper
3. Silastic basket
4. Metalized foil

Keep in mind that regular maintenance will extend the life of your air fryer. Your air fryer may malfunction and produce food with a poor flavour if it is not clean. Or even worse, it might cause a kitchen fire.

Are Air Fryers Safe?

Absolutely! They are secure and safe. To use your air fryer effectively and safely, you just need to abide by the following guidelines:

- Never set your air fryer on a stovetop, even if it almost cooled down.
- Sit your air fryer on a surface that can withstand heat. You might need to purchase a rolling tray or silicone mat to protect your counters if you don't have one, depending on the material of your countertops.
- When cooking, keep your air fryer 15-30 cm away from the wall. Position the air fryer at least 30 cm away from any wall outlets if you're cooking close to them because the air fryer's back can get quite hot.
- Use silicone tongs or a long oven mitt to remove food from the air fryer to avoid scorching your hands and forearms.
- After each use, make sure you disconnect your air fryer.
- Always let the air fryer cool completely before cleaning.
- Never dip the cooking unit or plugs in water. It will damage your air fryer.

Differences Between a Deep Fryer and an Air Fryer

While deep fryers cook food in a vat of oil that has been heated to a specified temperature, air fryers cook food at high temperatures with a hot air blowing mechanism.

Both cook food rapidly, but a deep fryer might take up to 10 minutes to fully heat up the oil in comparison to an air fryer, which takes virtually none.

In comparison to deep fryers, which use a lot of oil that absorbs into the food, air fryers likewise use little to no oil that leaves food feeling crispier.

Both appliances produce juicy, crispy food, but the food doesn't taste the same. This is typically because deep-fried foods are covered in batter, which would cook opposingly in an air fryer than in a deep fryer.

While the batter soaks hot oil in a deep fryer, battered dishes need to be misted with oil before they are cooked in an air fryer to help them colour and get crispy.

Wet batters made with flour don't cook properly in the air fryer, but would do in a deep fryer.

Are Air Fryers Worth it?

Consider whether you need a new appliance before anything else. Today, many toaster ovens and some pressure cookers are equipped with air frying capabilities.

If you do decide to invest in an air fryer, keep in mind that they can cost anywhere from £50 for small, portable models to £400 for larger, toaster oven-style air fryers.

If you're buying an air fryer, think about who you'll be feeding: The smallest air fryers, measuring 1.2 litres, are suitable for 1-2 people, while the medium-sized ones, measuring 3-4 litres, are suitable for 2-3 people, and the larger ones, measuring 6 litres or more, are suitable for 4-6 people.

Because they cook more evenly, air fryers with baskets are preferred over those with shelves.

Foods to Avoid Cooking in Air Fryer

BATTERED FOODS

Don't cook wet batter in the air fryer. A mess would be created and the dish won't crisp up well since wet batter wouldn't set like it would when immersed in oil. Coat your dish in flour, egg, and breadcrumbs to add a little crispiness and get it perfectly brown every time. Having said that, it is acceptable to use the air fryer to cook pre-fried, frozen food that has been battered.

FRESH LEAFY GREENS

The machine employs high-speed air, which will cause leafy greens like spinach to cook unevenly. Foods that don't stay in place are incredibly simple to burn. Choose veggies with some weight, such as broccoli and courgette, when cooking them in the air fryer. If you coat the kale in enough oil to weigh the leaves down, kale chips might also turn out well. Ultimately, frozen vegetables are best for air fryers because moisture is retained from the ice.

ROASTS

The biggest concern when using an air fryer to prepare a whole roast is whether or not the roast will fit completely inside the air fryer's basket. However, it's preferable to just stick to the standard oven even if the meat does fit.

The roast won't cook evenly, and by the time the portion furthest from the heat is safe to eat, the portion closest to the heat source will probably burn.

Everything comes down to crowding. Cooking the roast in smaller portions is preferable since the hot air requires space to flow properly.

CHEESE

Who wouldn't enjoy making some fried cheese right away? Unfortunately, since your air fryer isn't actually cooking your food, cheese placed inside will just melt into a puddle and make a mess that you don't want to clean up. For the best fried cheese option, try using frozen mozzarella sticks.

This also holds true with grilling cheese because it will probably burn due to the high pressure of the hot air. For this traditional comfort dish, stick to the stovetop or grill.

RAW GRAINS

Rice and pasta must first be cooked on the stovetop before they can be crisped in an air fryer. It won't work to try to cook something that has to be submerged in water because air fryers are designed to cook food dry. Even if your air fryer has a water reservoir, the fan will never get hot enough to boil the water and cook your grains.

HAMBURGERS

If you prefer your burgers medium-rare, air fryers aren't actually made for grilling red meat. The outside of the burger may not brown as fast as desired even though an air fryer cooks meat to medium-rare in a relatively short period of time. An air fryer won't give your steak the sear that balances it out if you prefer it red and juicy. However, if you need your burgers extremely well done, an air fryer should work just well.

TOAST

In theory, an air fryer's evenly dispersed hot air should be able to toast a slice of bread rather nicely. In fact, bread will move about and scatter crumbs all over the basket because of the strong air pressure in an air fryer, despite claims made that the appliance can toast bread. Keep in mind that an air fryer is not the same as a toaster oven. If you want a crispy piece of bread, stick to toasters and toaster ovens.

POPCORN

Before placing in an air fryer, microwave popcorn and packaged, ready-to-eat popcorn bags. Although an air fryer chamber may resemble a closed pot, they usually don't become hot enough to pop popcorn. Normal air fryer temperatures range from 150-200°C, but popping popcorn necessitates temperatures between 200 and 230°C.

Energy Efficiency of Air Fryers

Because they are smaller appliances, air fryers often use less energy and less electricity than conventional ovens. Because the heating element in an air fryer is placed closer to the food and circulates hot air in a condensed area, your food will cook quicker than it would in an oven and won't require preheating.

However, an air fryer might not be a money saver if you need to cook many batches of food to finish your meal. Instead, using your oven might be more time and energy efficient.

To save energy, always turn off the air fryer at the outlet when it's not in use. Appliances that are left on at the outlet are hidden energy consumers.

In this book, you will learn how to make 100 Air Fryer-friendly recipes that you and your loved ones will love to eat.

About the Author

A group of Chefs trying to make cooking fun and healthy again!

We know how busy you are, that is why we aim to make our recipes as easy, budget friendly and delicious as possible, so you can cook up meals you look forward to that nourish you simultaneously.

With every book we create we also include a Bonus PDF so you get access to coloured images with every single recipe! We couldn't include them in the book due to printing costs and we wanted to keep the books as affordable as possible. We hope you enjoy!

Please email us & our customer support team will help as soon as we possibly can! We want to make sure you are 100% satisfied and if you have any issues at all please email us and we will do our best to help.

Also, if you have any feedback on how we can improve this book & further books please email us that and we will make all the changes we can. As mentioned we can't add colour photos inside the book due to printing costs, but any other improvements we would love to make!

Our customer support email is

✉ **vicandersonpublishing@gmail.com**

As mentioned, email us anything you wish here.

Please scan the QR code below to access your bonus PDF with all 150 recipes with full coloured photos & beautiful designs alongside! This is the only way we can get the recipes with coloured photos to you & keep the book as reasonably priced as possible.

Also, once downloaded you can take the PDF with you digitally wherever you go- meaning you can cook these recipes wherever you may be! (As long as you have an air fryer!)

We hope you enjoy and do let us know your feedback!

STEP BY STEP GUIDE TO ACCESS

1. Open Your Phones (Or Any Device You Want The Book On) Back Camera. The Back Camera Is The One You use as if you are taking a picture of someone.
2. Simply point your Camera at the QR code and 'tap' the QR code with your finger to focus the camera.
3. A link / pop up will appear. Simply tap that (and make sure you have internet connection) and the FREE PDF containing all of the coloured images should appear.
4. Now you have access to these FOREVER. Simply 'Bookmark' The tab it opened on, or download the document and take wherever you want.
5. Repeat this on any device you want it on! (If you want it on a laptop, simply email the document to yourself!)

Any issues please email us at:
vicandersonpublishing@gmail.com
and we will be happy to help!!

Breakfast
Recipes

BACON, CHICKEN ROLL UPS

Bacon, chicken roll ups is a tasty low-carb meal with only a few ingredients. It is a delicious option to kickstart the morning yet comfy on the tummy. Making chicken roll-ups from boneless chicken breast is simple. And what's better, they are wrapped in bacon for that extra pack of flavour and taste.

 PREPARATION TIME: **10 MINUTES** | COOKING TIME: **15 MINUTES**

SERVING SIZE: **2** | PER SERVING: **KCAL: 458; FAT: 3-G; CARBS: 5G; PROTEIN: 41G; SUGARS: 2G; FIBRE: 0G**

Ingredients:

- 1 fillet of chicken breast, skinless and boneless
- 40g can creamed sweetcorn
- 60g soft cheese, diced, at room temperature
- 40g grated three-cheese mix, of choice
- 1 tbsp. chopped fresh coriander
- 2 rashers of streaky bacon
- Tomato salsa for serving
- Cooking oil for coating

Instructions:

Step 1: Preheat the air fryer to 180°C.

Step 2: Slice the chicken breast in halves lengthwise and using a mallet, pound both to 5-mm thickness.

Step 3: In a bowl, mix the creamed corn, soft cheese, cheese mix, and coriander. Divide the mixture onto both chicken pieces. Gently roll the chicken over the filling, wrap each with one bacon, and secure the ends with toothpicks.

Step 4: Lightly coat the air fryer's basket with cooking oil and place the wrapped chicken in it. Air fry at 180°C for 15 minutes, turning halfway through cooking or until golden.

Step 5: Remove them onto a plate, remove the toothpicks, and serve with tomato salsa.

BAKED PESTO EGGS

Here is a fine trick for creating some character in the morning and giving everyone a pleasant surprise. They are healthy too! This six-ingredient breakfast or brunch with spinach, basil pesto, and bubbling melted cheese is ready in less than 25 minutes.

 PREPARATION TIME: **10 MINUTES** | COOKING TIME: **12 MINUTES**

SERVING SIZE: **2** | PER SERVING: **KCAL: 245; FAT: 22G; CARBS: 3G; PROTEIN: 10G; SUGARS: 1G; FIBRE: 1G**

Ingredients:

- 4 tbsp. roughly chopped baby spinach
- 1 tbsp. fresh basil pesto
- 4 tbsp. double cream
- Salt and black pepper to taste
- 1 tbsp. finely grated Gruyère cheese
- 2 medium eggs

Instructions:

Step 1: Preheat the air fryer to 200°C.

Step 2: In a bowl, combine the spinach, pesto, double cream, salt, and black pepper.

Step 3: Divide the mixture into two small shallow ovenproof dishes. Sprinkle the cheese on top.

Step 4: Make a shallow well in both mixtures and crack an egg into each hole.

Step 5: Bake them in the air fryer for 10 to 12 minutes or until the egg whites set and the yolks are runny.

Step 6: Take them out and serve them warm.

BEANS AND CHEESE ON TOAST

A quick and easy toast recipe loaded with beans but enhanced with tomato sauce and cheese. Use your preferred beans, along with some garlic tomato sauce, chilli, and other seasonings (as preferred) to create an improved version of beans on toast. They taste fantastic with a melt of cheese on top.

PREPARATION TIME: **10 MINUTES** | COOKING TIME: **18 MINUTES**

SERVING SIZE: **2** | PER SERVING: **KCAL: 327; FAT: 12G; CARBS: 42G; PROTEIN: 15G; SUGARS: 11G; FIBRE: 6G**

Ingredients:

- Cooking oil for coating
- 1 large onion, finely chopped
- 4 garlic cloves, finely chopped
- 100g small grape tomatoes, halved or quartered
- Salt and black pepper to taste
- 1 tsp. smoked paprika, plus extra for sprinkling
- 1 tsp. ground cumin
- Red chilli flakes to taste
- 100g can baked beans (or other beans of choice), pre-warmed on a stove.
- 4 slices crusty bread
- 4 tbsp. grated cheddar

Instructions:

Step 1: Preheat the air fryer to 190°C.

Step 2: Coat the air fryer basket with a little cooking oil and spread in the onion, garlic, and tomatoes. Season with salt, black pepper, paprika, and cumin. Roast for 10 minutes.

Step 3: Transfer the mixture to a blender, add the chilli flakes and blend until smooth. Season to taste.

Step 4: Toast the bread slices for 2 minutes per side or until they are golden brown. Place them on a plate.

Step 5: On two bread pieces, spread some of the tomato sauce, then some warmed beans, and finally the cheese. Cover with the other two bread slices.

Step 6: Gently place them in the air fryer and toast them for 1 to 2 more minutes or until the cheese melts.

Step 7: Serve the toast warm.

BREAKFAST EGG SALSA

Simple additions transform regular eggs into extraordinary ones! You prepare some scrambled eggs, add some coriander, salsa, and cheese, and there, you transform simplicity into something great.

PREPARATION TIME: **10 MINUTES** | COOKING TIME: **11 MINUTES**

SERVING SIZE: **2** | PER SERVING: **KCAL: 895; FAT: 75G; CARBS: 4G; PROTEIN: 50G; SUGARS: 2G; FIBRE: 0G**

Ingredients:

- 200g thick pork sausages
- 1 tbsp. chopped fresh green onions
- 120g of sharp cheddar cheese, grated
- 120g Monterey Jack cheese, grated
- 2 large eggs, beaten
- 1 tbsp. semi-skimmed milk
- ½ tsp. of salt or to taste
- ½ tsp. black pepper or to taste
- Salsa for topping

Instructions:

Step 1: Preheat the air fryer to 200°C.

Step 2: Cook the sausage in a skillet over medium heat for 4 to 6 minutes. Stir often while breaking up the sausage until it is no longer pink. Add the green onions, and both cheeses. Stir until the cheeses have melted.

Step 3: Crack the eggs into a bowl and whisk with milk, salt, and black pepper.

Step 4: Spread the sausage mixture on a small egg pan (designed for the air fryer). Place the pan in the air fryer and pour on the egg.

Step 5: Cook for 4 to 5 minutes while stirring every 1 minute or until the eggs have scrambled.

Step 6: Take out the griddle pan and top the eggs with salsa.

Step 7: Serve warm.

EGGY CHEESE CRUMPETS

Switch to these delectable eggy cheese crumpets for breakfast instead of your usual toast or sandwiches. Enjoy them with sliced avocado and cherry tomatoes. These open crumpets are quickly prepared, delicious, and cheesy.

PREPARATION TIME: **10 MINUTES** | COOKING TIME: **8 MINUTES**

SERVING SIZE: **2** | PER SERVING: **KCAL: 989; FAT: 55G; CARBS: 102G; PROTEIN: 25G; SUGARS: 8G; FIBRE: 10G**

Ingredients:

- 2 eggs
- 4 tbsp. milk
- 4 crumpets, split
- 4 tbsp. cherry tomatoes, halved
- A drizzle of vegetable oil
- 1 tbsp. grated cheddar
- 1 small ripe avocado, pitted, peeled, and sliced

Instructions:

Step 1: Preheat the air fryer to 190°C.

Step 2: Crack the eggs into a bowl and whisk with the milk until smooth. Dip the crumpets into the eggs on both sides and let them sit in the eggs for 5 minutes.

Step 3: Coat the air fryer basket with a little cooking oil and place the crumpets in it (open side facing downwards). Cook for 3 to 4 minutes per side or until they set.

Step 4: On the second turn, place the tomatoes by the sides of the crumpets and let them brown along. Also, sprinkle the cheese on top and let them melt.

Step 5: Plate the crumpets with the open side facing upwards and top with the tomatoes.

Step 6: Add the avocado slices on top and serve.

CHOCOLATE BREAD PUDDING

Dating as far back as I can remember, this dish was a regular in my home as a child. We even served it at brunch, dessert on some days, and my mother made sure to make an impression with it on special occasions. Such a canvas, you can throw in just about any sweet ingredient. It is the ultimate way to use bread scraps too. It is straightforward to prepare and with a helping of vanilla ice cream, you have yourself a delicious dessert too.

 PREPARATION TIME: **20 MINUTES** | COOKING TIME: **13 MINUTES**

 SERVING SIZE: **2** | PER SERVING: **KCAL: 528; FAT: 16G; CARBS: 88G; PROTEIN: 10G; SUGARS: 73G; FIBRE: 2G**

Ingredients:

- 4 tbsp. chopped semisweet chocolate
- 150 ml single cream
- 100g granulated sugar
- 1 large egg, beaten
- 140 ml semi-skimmed milk
- 1 tsp. vanilla extract
- ¼ tsp. salt
- 2 pieces of day-old bread, crusts removed and cubed
- Icing sugar for garnish

Instructions:

Step 1: Preheat the air fryer to 160°C.

Step 2: Combine the chocolate and single cream in a microwave-safe bowl and microwave for a few seconds until the chocolate melts. Take out the bowl and mix until smooth and silky.

Step 3: In a larger bowl, whisk the sugar, egg, milk, vanilla, and salt until smooth. Stir in the chocolate mixture until smooth. Add the bread cubes and coat them well. Let stand for 15 minutes to allow the bread to soak the chocolate mixture.

Step 4: Spoon the mixture into two medium ramekins.

Step 5: Place the ramekins in the air fryer and bake for 12 to 15 minutes or until set at the centre.

Step 6: Remove the ramekins and sprinkle the tops with icing sugar.

Step 7: Serve warm.

FRENCH TOAST STICKS

These bite-sized French toast sticks gleam with sugar and cinnamon, and they are perfectly dippable in a sweet sauce. Kids and adults alike will have a thrill with them. For the best taste, have the bread dipped in the sweet egg mix until they are so soaked. After cooking, dust them richly with cinnamon sugar, and drizzle on some melted butter. You can thank me later.

⏱ PREPARATION TIME: **10 MINUTES** | 🍲 COOKING TIME: **6 MINUTES**

🍽 SERVING SIZE: **2** | PER SERVING: **KCAL: 357; FAT: 7G; CARBS: 62G; PROTEIN: 11G; SUGARS: 6G; FIBRE: 6G**

Ingredients:

- 2 slices of day-old bread
- 1 large egg
- 120 ml semi-skimmed milk
- ½ tsp. sugar
- 1 tsp. vanilla extract
- 1 tsp. of cinnamon powder
- 120g crumbled cornflakes (optional)
- Maple syrup for serving

Instructions:

Step 1: Preheat the air fryer to 180°C.

Step 2: Cut each bread slice into three strips.

Step 3: Crack the egg into a bowl and whisk with the milk, sugar, vanilla, and cinnamon until smooth. Dip the bread strips in the egg mixture and let them soak for 3 minutes on each side.

Step 4: After, coat the bread pieces in the cornflakes on both sides (this step is optional).

Step 5: Grease the air fryer basket with a little cooking oil and air fry the bread sticks for 2 to 3 minutes per side or until they are golden brown.

Step 6: Transfer them to a plate, drizzle on some maple syrup, and serve warm.

HASH BROWN EGG BITES

The hash brown potato crust gives these egg pieces plenty of crunch. Fresh hash browns, which can be purchased in the vegetable area of most supermarkets, guarantee a crispier end product than frozen ones. Additionally, drying them out before baking removes extra moisture, guaranteeing an even crispier result.

⏱ PREPARATION TIME: **10 MINUTES** | 🍲 COOKING TIME: **12 MINUTES**

🍽 SERVING SIZE: **2** | PER SERVING: **KCAL: 771; FAT: 61G; CARBS: 21G; PROTEIN: 36G; SUGARS: 2G; FIBRE: 2G**

Ingredients:

- 2 large eggs
- 4 tbsp. double cream
- Rock salt and black pepper to taste
- 2 tbsp. grated cheddar
- 2 tbsp. chopped red bell pepper
- 1 scallion, white and green parts chopped separately
- 120g frozen (thawed) or freshly made hash browns

Instructions:

Step 1: Preheat the air fryer to 180°C.

Step 2: Grease an 8-holed egg mould with cooking spray and line each hole with hash browns. Set aside.

Step 3: Crack the eggs into a bowl and whisk with the double cream, salt, and black pepper. Add the cheddar cheese, bell pepper, and scallion. Mix well.

Step 4: Spoon the egg mixture into the silicone mould on top of the hash browns.

Step 5: Place the mould in the air fryer and bake for 10 to 12 minutes or until the eggs set and the hash browns are golden.

Step 6: Remove the egg mould and let it cool to touch.

Step 7: Pop out the egg bites and enjoy.

HAM, CHEESE, AND EGG POCKETS

These delectable ham, egg, and cheese pockets are easy to make in 15 minutes, won't leave a trace of mess behind, and have a crispy outside and melty inside. There's no need to make dough from scratch. Grab a portion from the store and fill them up with ham, cheese, and egg.

⏱ PREPARATION TIME: **10 MINUTES** | 🍲 COOKING TIME: **15 MINUTES**

🍽 SERVING SIZE: **2** | PER SERVING: **KCAL: 740; FAT: 56G; CARBS: 43G; PROTEIN: 18G; SUGARS: 1G; FIBRE: 2G**

Ingredients:

- 1 large egg
- 2 tsp. semi-skimmed milk
- Salt and black pepper to taste
- 2 tbsp. butter, melted
- 2 deli ham slices, chopped
- 2 tbsp. grated cheddar cheese
- 1 pack of chilled croissant dough

Instructions:

Step 1: Preheat the air fryer to 170°C.

Step 2: Crack the egg into a bowl and whisk with the milk, salt, and black pepper until smooth.

Step 3: Grease a small egg pan (for the air fryer) with 1 tbsp. of butter and pour the egg in it. Cook in the air fryer for 3 to 4 minutes while stirring every 1 minute until the eggs are scrambled. Take out the pan.

Step 4: Create two rectangles from the dough. Divide the scrambled egg at the centre of each and top with the ham, and cheddar cheese. Fold one end of each dough piece over the filling and crimp their ends to seal. Brush the top with the remaining butter.

Step 5: Place the pockets in the air fryer and bake for 8 to 10 minutes or until golden brown.

Step 6: Take them out and let cool to your liking.

Step 7: Serve.

SCOTCH EGGS

Scotch eggs, a gastropub speciality, capture my heart every time. It is a nice juggle between breakfast, brunch, and a snack option. How versatile! It is merely cooked eggs wrapped in sausage meat and then breaded and fried. This recipe keeps things simple and I hope it will be as breezy for you.

⏱ PREPARATION TIME: **10 MINUTES** | 🍲 COOKING TIME: **15 MINUTES**

🍽 SERVING SIZE: **2** | PER SERVING: **KCAL: 932; FAT: 50G; CARBS: 79G; PROTEIN: 41G; SUGARS: 1G; FIBRE: 7G**

Ingredients:

- 200g thick pork sausages
- Salt and black pepper to taste
- 6 large hard-boiled eggs, peeled
- 1 large egg, lightly beaten
- 200g cornflakes, finely crumbled

Instructions:

Step 1: Preheat the air fryer to 200°C.

Step 2: Season the pork sausage with salt and black pepper, and mix well.

Step 3: Wrap each egg with pork sausage and press to firmly hold. Dip the wrapped egg in the beaten egg and coat well with the cornflakes.

Step 4: Grease the air fryer basket with a little cooking oil and arrange the eggs in it.

Step 5: Air fry for 12 to 15 minutes or until golden and the meat is no longer pink while turning around every 3 to 4 minutes.

Step 6: Plate the scotch eggs and serve them warm.

SAUSAGE AND POTATO

Sausage and potatoes in 20 minutes? How is that even possible? Thanks to the air fryer, this tasty and simple breakfast cooks to perfection. It is such a comfort food that gives you room to season it with anything that you like. Garlic and herbs work for me but some chilli would be a nice kick too.

⏱ PREPARATION TIME: **15 MINUTES** | 🍲 COOKING TIME: **20 MINUTES**

🍽 SERVING SIZE: **2** | PER SERVING: **KCAL: 793; FAT: 51G; CARBS: 58G; PROTEIN: 26G; SUGARS: 10G; FIBRE: 9G**

Ingredients:

- 450g potatoes, peeled and diced
- 1 tsp. olive oil
- 300g smoked sausage, cut into 30 cm slices
- 1 red or green bell pepper, deseeded and chopped
- 1 large red onion, diced
- 200g grape tomatoes
- 1 tbsp. crumbled feta cheese

For seasoning:

- 1 tbsp. olive oil
- 2 garlic cloves, minced
- 2 tsp. fresh lemon juice
- 1 tsp. dried oregano
- Salt to taste
- ½ tsp. black pepper
- 1 tsp. fresh lemon zest

Instructions:

Step 1: Preheat the air fryer to 200°C.

Step 2: In a small bowl, combine the seasoning ingredients and set aside.

Step 3: Add the potatoes to a bowl with half of the seasoning mix and olive oil. Toss well.

Step 4: Pour the mixture into the air fryer and cook for 15 minutes or until nearly done.

Step 5: Add the sausage, onion, bell pepper, and remaining seasoning mix to the potatoes. Toss well and cook for 3 more minutes or until the sausages are fork tender.

Step 6: Stir in the tomatoes and feta cheese. Cook for 2 more minutes.

Step 7: Spoon into a serving bowl and serve warm.

SHAKSHUKA

In Israel, North Africa, and other Middle Eastern countries, shakshuka is well-enjoyed for breakfast or at other times of the day. You can alter its flavour as you like—think pesto, curry powder, fresh herbs. Simply simmer some tomatoes, onions, garlic, and spices and gently poach some eggs in the sauce.

PREPARATION TIME: **10 MINUTES** | COOKING TIME: **12 MINUTES**

SERVING SIZE: **2** | PER SERVING: **KCAL: 199; FAT: 11G; CARBS: 18G; PROTEIN: 8G; SUGARS: 10G; FIBRE: 4G**

Ingredients:

- 1 tbsp. olive oil
- 2 red onions, chopped
- 1 red chilli, deseeded and finely chopped
- 1 garlic clove, sliced
- 200g cherry tomatoes
- A small bunch coriander stalks and leaves chopped separately
- 1 tsp. caster sugar
- Salt and black pepper to taste
- 2 eggs

Instructions:

Step 1: Preheat the air fryer to 190°C.

Step 2: In a medium cooking pan (for the air fryer), spread the olive oil and add the onion, chilli, and garlic. Cook in the air fryer for 2 minutes.

Step 3: Pour on the tomatoes, coriander stalks, and season with sugar, salt and black pepper. Cook for 4 to 5 minutes or until the tomatoes are tender.

Step 4: Create two holes in the sauce and crack an egg into each hole. Lightly season the eggs with salt and black pepper. Cook for 4 to 5 minutes or until the eggs set to your desired tastes.

Step 5: Take out the pan and garnish with coriander. Serve warm with crusty bread.

SPINACH AND CHEESE FRITTATA

You might not have considered making a frittata in your air fryer, but you can! You'll get a beautiful brown crust with a creamy interior, and the clever use of a springform cake pan makes unmoulding a breeze.

⏱ PREPARATION TIME: **10 MINUTES** | 🍲 COOKING TIME: **10 MINUTES**

🍽 SERVING SIZE: **2** | PER SERVING: **KCAL: 404; FAT: 30G; CARBS: 8G; PROTEIN: 26G; SUGARS: 3G; FIBRE: 3G**

Ingredients:

- 2 large eggs
- 2 tbsp. double cream
- Salt and black pepper to taste
- 1 small each red, yellow, or orange bell pepper, chopped
- 110g baby spinach leaves, loosely packed and roughly chopped
- 2 scallions, finely chopped
- 2 tbsp. chopped fresh basil
- 2 tbsp. fresh Italian parsley, chopped
- 120g mild cheddar cheese, grated
- 2 tbsp. grated Parmesan cheese

Instructions:

Step 1: Preheat the air fryer to 160°C.

Step 2: Grease a 10-cm springform pan with cooking spray.

Step 3: Crack the eggs into a bowl and whisk with the double cream, salt, and black pepper. Add the bell pepper, spinach, scallions, basil, parsley, and half of the cheese. Mix well and sprinkle the remaining cheeses on top.

Step 4: Place the pan in the air fryer and bake for 10 minutes or until the eggs are cooked when tested with a toothpick.

Step 5: Take out the pan, let rest for 3 to 5 minutes, and release the pan. Slice and serve warm.

SPINACH AND MUSHROOM QUICHE

This healthy vegetarian quiche recipe is as effortless as it gets. It's quiche without the fussy crust. Filled with sweet wild mushrooms and savoury Gruyère cheese, you will wish to eat it every day. Pack up a wedge to work and enjoy it with a light salad for lunch.

PREPARATION TIME: **15 MINUTES** | COOKING TIME: **14 MINUTES**

SERVING SIZE: **2** | PER SERVING: **KCAL: 589; FAT: 49G; CARBS: 15G; PROTEIN: 23G; SUGARS: 13G; FIBRE: 1G**

Ingredients:

- 1 tbsp. olive oil
- 50g sliced fresh mixed wild mushrooms (such as cremini, shiitake, button and/or oyster mushrooms)
- 2 tbsp. thinly sliced sweet onion
- 1 tsp. thinly sliced garlic
- 4 tbsp. fresh baby spinach, coarsely chopped
- 2 large eggs
- 2 tbsp. full-fat milk
- 2 tbsp. single cream
- 1 tsp. English mustard
- 1 tsp. chopped fresh thyme leaves, plus more for garnish
- ½ tsp. salt or to taste
- ½ tsp. black pepper or to taste
- 4 tbsp. grated Gruyère cheese

Instructions:

Step 1: Preheat the air fryer to 180°C.

Step 2: Coat a 20-cm pie pan with cooking spray and set it aside.

Step 3: Heat the olive oil in a skillet over medium heat (on a stovetop) and sauté the mushrooms for 8 minutes or until the liquid has evaporated and they are tender. Add the onion and cook for 3 minutes or until tender. Add the garlic and cook for 1 minute or until fragrant. Stir in the spinach and cook for 2 minutes or until wilted. Set aside.

Step 4: Crack the eggs into a bowl and whisk with the milk, cream, English mustard, thyme, salt, and black pepper until smooth. Add the mushroom mixture and mix well.

Step 5: Pour the egg mixture into the pie pan and use a spoon to spread it out evenly. Sprinkle the Gruyère cheese on top.

Step 6: Place the pan in the air fryer and bake for 25 to 30 minutes or until golden brown on top and around the edges.

Step 7: Take out the pie pan, garnish with thyme, and let it rest for 5 minutes.

Step 8: Slice and serve the quiche warm.

TACOS TWIST

Who said you can't have tacos for breakfast? This twist (pun intended) of a taco gives you delicious and crunchy goodness right at the day's start. These taco twists are seasoned beef baked in twisted flaky dough. They are particularly great for kids.

PREPARATION TIME: 20 MINUTES | **COOKING TIME: 22 MINUTES**

SERVING SIZE: 2 | PER SERVING: **KCAL: 1500; FAT: 108G; CARBS: 65G; PROTEIN: 70G; SUGARS: 5G; FIBRE: 5G**

Ingredients:

- 300g beef mince
- 1 large onion, chopped
- 250g grated cheddar
- 2 tbsp. salsa
- 1 tbsp. chopped canned green chilies
- ½ tsp. garlic powder
- ¼ tsp. hot sauce
- ½ tsp. salt or to taste
- ½ tsp. ground cumin
- 240g chilled croissant dough
- Optional toppings: chopped tomatoes, ripe olives, shredded lettuce, and sliced jalapeño peppers

Instructions:

Step 1: Preheat the air fryer to 150°C.

Step 2: Cook the beef and onion in a skillet over medium heat for 10 minutes until the meat is no longer pink. Break up the meat with your spoon as it cooks. Drain the resulting liquid from the meat.

Step 3: Turn the heat off and stir in the cheddar, salsa, chillies, garlic powder, hot sauce, salt, and cumin.

Step 4: Roll out the dough and divide into four rectangles; press the dough to seal any holes.

Step 5: Add half of the meat mixture to the centre of each rectangle. Twist all four corners together and then squeeze them together to seal.

Step 6: Coat the air fryer basket with a little cooking oil and place the taco twists in it in a single layer.

Step 7: Air fry them for 18 to 22 minutes or until they are golden brown.

Step 8: Take them out, add any taco toppings that you'd like, and serve them warm.

SCAN ME

Please scan the QR code below to access your bonus PDF with all 150 recipes with full coloured photos & beautiful designs alongside! This is the only way we can get the recipes with coloured photos to you & keep the book as reasonably priced as possible.

Also, once downloaded you can take the PDF with you digitally wherever you go- meaning you can cook these recipes wherever you may be! (As long as you have an air fryer!)

We hope you enjoy and do let us know your feedback!

STEP BY STEP GUIDE TO ACCESS

1. Open Your Phones (Or Any Device You Want The Book On) Back Camera. The Back Camera Is The One You use as if you are taking a picture of someone.
2. Simply point your Camera at the QR code and 'tap' the QR code with your finger to focus the camera.
3. A link / pop up will appear. Simply tap that (and make sure you have internet connection) and the FREE PDF containing all of the coloured images should appear.
4. Now you have access to these FOREVER. Simply 'Bookmark' The tab it opened on, or download the document and take wherever you want.
5. Repeat this on any device you want it on! (If you want it on a laptop, simply email the document to yourself!)

Any issues please email us at:
vicandersonpublishing@gmail.com
and we will be happy to help!!

Lunch Recipes

BONE-IN PORK CHOPS WITH SWEET RHUBARB SAUCE

Pork chops are delicious and because they are straightforward and quick to cook, they are perfect for lunch. This recipe comes with a sweet rhubarb sauce topping and serves well with vegetables, chips, and rice.

PREPARATION TIME: 10 MINUTES | **COOKING TIME: 18 MINUTES**

SERVING SIZE: 2 | PER SERVING: **KCAL: 312; FAT: 13G; CARBS: 8G; PROTEIN: 40G; SUGARS: 4G; FIBRE: 2G**

Ingredients:

- 2 bone-in, 2-cm-thick pork loin chops
- ½ tsp. salt or to taste
- ½ tsp. black pepper or to taste
- 1 tbsp. butter
- 200g rhubarb, fresh or frozen, chopped
- 1 tsp. honey
- ½ tsp. cinnamon powder
- ½ tsp. minced fresh parsley

Instructions:

Step 1: Preheat the air fryer to 200°C.

Step 2: Season the pork chops with salt and black pepper. Place them in the air fryer and cook for 4 to 5 minutes per side or until they are golden and reach an internal temperature of 63°C.

Step 3: Meanwhile, melt the butter in a skillet over medium heat. Add the rhubarb and let cook for 5 minutes. Stir in the honey and cinnamon. Simmer for 2 to 3 minutes or until the rhubarb is very tender.

Step 4: Take out the pork chops when ready and let them rest for 5 to 10 minutes.

Step 5: Spoon the sweet rhubarb sauce over the pork and garnish with parsley.

Step 6: Serve warm.

CREAMY ROTISSERIE CHICKEN SALAD

I put a flavour twist on the classic chicken salad by using a lemon-herb mayonnaise. Try other mayo varieties, like roasted garlic or chilli lime. Serve this fast and warm rotisserie chicken salad fresh. It is perfect in sandwiches and wraps, and serves just as good by itself.

PREPARATION TIME: 10 MINUTES | **COOKING TIME: 5 MINUTES**

SERVING SIZE: 2 | PER SERVING: **KCAL: 123; FAT: 7G; CARBS: 1G; PROTEIN: 14G; SUGARS: 0G; FIBRE: 0G**

Ingredients:

- 100g chopped rotisserie chicken
- 1 tbsp. chopped celery
- 1 tbsp. lemon-herb mayonnaise
- Cracked black pepper to taste

Instructions:

Step 1: Preheat the air fryer to 190°C.

Step 2: Add the chicken and celery to the air fryer, and warm for 5 minutes.

Step 3: Transfer the chicken mixture to a bowl and top with the lemon-herb mayonnaise and black pepper. Mix well and serve.

BULGOGI WITH COURGETTE

I love this thinly sliced beef dish marinated in a sweet and flavourful sauce. Traditionally, they'll be cooked swiftly over flames with some courgette noodles to pair. But with the air fryer, I show you a fine trick to make it just as tasty. Make sure to make time to marinate the beef before cooking because that's the top note for its great taste.

 PREPARATION TIME: **2 HOURS 10 MINUTES** | COOKING TIME: **15 MINUTES**

SERVING SIZE: **2** | PER SERVING: **KCAL: 320; FAT: 19G; CARBS: 9G; PROTEIN: 29G; SUGARS: 6G; FIBRE: 0G**

Ingredients:

- 1 tbsp. soy sauce, low sodium
- 1 tbsp. sugar
- 2 tbsp. mirin
- 2 tbsp. toasted sesame oil
- 3 garlic cloves, minced
- Salt and black pepper to taste
- 1 large courgette, cut in halves lengthwise, then cut into 1 cm pieces
- 250g beef, preferably ribeye, thinly sliced
- Sesame seeds for garnish

Instructions:

Step 1: Preheat the air fryer to 200°C.

Step 2: In a bowl, combine the soy sauce, sugar, mirin, sesame oil, garlic, salt, and black pepper. Add the beef, stir well, and let marinate in the fridge for 2 hours.

Step 3: In a medium cooking pan (for the air fryer), spread the beef and cook in the air fryer for 10 minutes.

Step 4: Season the courgette with salt and black pepper. Add it to the beef, stir, and cook for 2 to 3 minutes or until the courgette is tender.

Step 5: Take out the pan and garnish the dish with sesame seeds.

Step 6: Serve warm with rice.

· ·

QUESADILLAS

Make a large batch of these simple quesadillas and since they freeze fantastically, you can preserve them for other week days. Serve them with soured cream, salsa, or avocado sauce.

 PREPARATION TIME: **5 MINUTES** | COOKING TIME: **14 MINUTES**

 SERVING SIZE: **2** | PER SERVING: **KCAL: 501; FAT: 23G; CARBS: 52G; PROTEIN: 22G; SUGARS: 5G; FIBRE: 3G**

Ingredients:

- 4 medium flour tortillas, warmed
- 4 tbsp. salsa
- 120g grated Mexican cheese blend

Instructions:

Step 1: Preheat the air fryer to 180°C.

Step 2: Lay two tortillas on a clean, flat surface. Divide and spread the salsa on top of them followed by the cheese mix. Cover each one with one tortilla.

Step 3: Working in batches, bake each set of tortillas in the air fryer for 5 to 7 minutes or until they are golden, crispy, and the cheeses have melted.

Step 4: Plate them and cut them into quarters to make 4 triangles.

Step 5: Serve warm. Freeze any extras and reheat in the air fryer when ready to enjoy.

CRANBERRY CHICKEN SALAD

This warm chicken salad with cranberries, toasty pecans, and softened vegetables is slathered in a mayonnaise and yoghurt dressing, which gives the salad an aroma that is utterly irresistible. Serve this delicious cranberry chicken salad open-face on toasted bread or pack it up on salad greens for a richer salad.

PREPARATION TIME: **10 MINUTES** | COOKING TIME: **8 MINUTES**

SERVING SIZE: **2** | PER SERVING: **KCAL: 329; FAT: 19G; CARBS: 16G; PROTEIN: 26G; SUGARS: 9G; FIBRE: 4G**

Ingredients:

- 4 tbsp. plain whole-milk yoghurt
- 2 tbsp. mayonnaise
- 2 tsp. chopped fresh scallions
- 1 tbsp. dill pickle relish
- 1 tbsp. English mustard
- ½ tsp. salt or to taste
- ½ tsp. black pepper or to taste
- 200g shredded cooked chicken breast
- 1 tbsp. sweetened dried cranberries
- 2 tbsp. chopped pecans, toasted
- 2 tsp. finely chopped celery
- 3 tbsp. finely chopped carrots

Instructions:

Step 1: Preheat the air fryer to 200°C.

Step 2: In a bowl, mix the yoghurt, mayonnaise, scallions, relish, mustard, salt, and black pepper. Set aside.

Step 3: Add the chicken, cranberries, pecans, celery, and carrot to the air fryer basket and mix well. Warm for 5 to 8 minutes or until the vegetables are partially tender.

Step 4: Transfer the chicken mixture to a bowl and mix in the yoghurt dressing.

Step 5: Serve warm.

DANISH GOZLEME

Whole feta and barely cooked spinach are placed inside this savoury Danish pastry. It has an attractive lattice on top that is simple to make. The crust cooks to such perfect crunch and is golden to whet your appetite in an instance. The filling is rich with partially melted feta, making it an excellent light lunch.

⏱ PREPARATION TIME: **15 MINUTES** | 🍲 COOKING TIME: **21 MINUTES**

🍽 SERVING SIZE: **2** | PER SERVING: **KCAL: 459; FAT: 35G; CARBS: 18G; PROTEIN: 19G; SUGARS: 5G; FIBRE: 2G**

Ingredients:

- 1 tsp. olive oil
- ¼ medium brown onion, finely chopped
- 80g frozen spinach, thawed with excess water squeezed out
- Salt and black pepper to taste
- 1 sheet of frozen puff pastry, thawed
- 200g Danish feta, cut in half horizontally
- 1 egg yolk, lightly whisked
- Lemon wedges for serving (optional)

Instructions:

Step 1: Preheat the air fryer to 180°C.

Step 2: Heat the olive oil in a skillet over medium heat and sauté the onion for 3 minutes. Add the spinach and cook for 2 to 3 minutes or until wilted. Season with salt and black pepper.

Step 3: Lay out the puff pastry and spread the feta in the centre. Add the spinach mixture on top.

Step 4: Along the pastry's long sides, diagonally cut 2-cm-wide strips and then, the short sides in halves. Starting with the short ends, overlap each side's halves over the filling. Then, overlap the strips for the long sides over the filling as well. You should have a lattice formed on top when done.

Step 5: Brush the pastry with egg and place it in the air fryer. Bake for 15 minutes or until golden and crisp.

Step 6: Take out the pastry, slice, and serve with lemon wedges.

FISH AND CHIPS

Most people can't help but like the traditional fish and chips, which is a British national dish. This simple recipe for beer-battered fish and chips has an outer that is wonderfully crispy and an interior that is soft and flaky. For a truly outstanding lunch, serve it with homemade tartar sauce.

PREPARATION TIME: **15 MINUTES** | COOKING TIME: **18 MINUTES**

SERVING SIZE: **2** | PER SERVING: **KCAL: 473; FAT: 18G; CARBS: 36G; PROTEIN: 40G; SUGARS: 1G; FIBRE: 3G**

Ingredients:

For the potatoes:

- 1 medium potato, peeled and cut into 1 cm strips
- 2 tbsp. olive oil
- Salt and black pepper to taste
- 4 tbsp. plain flour

For the fish:

- 1 large egg
- 2 tbsp. water
- 1 ½ tbsp. plain flour
- Salt and black pepper to taste
- 1 tbsp. grated Parmesan cheese
- 1 tsp. cayenne pepper
- 2 cod or haddock fillets
- Tartare sauce for serving (optional)

Instructions:

Step 1: Preheat the air fryer to 200°C.

For the potatoes:

Step 2: In a bowl, toss the potatoes with olive oil, salt, black pepper, and flour. Air fry the potatoes for 5 to 10 minutes or until golden and cooked within; shaking the basket once or twice through cooking.

For the fish:

Step 3: Crack the egg into a bowl and whisk with the water, flour, salt, black pepper, Parmesan cheese, and cayenne pepper.

Step 4: Dip the fish fillets in the batter to coat well. Place them on a plate and freeze until the potatoes are ready or until the batter is no longer runny.

Step 5: Transfer the potatoes to a plate when they are ready and place the battered fish in the air fryer in a single layer. Air fry them for 5 to 8 minutes or until they are golden and the fish is flaky.

Step 6: Plate the fish with the potatoes.

Step 7: Serve warm with tartar sauce.

SALTIMBOCCA

A classic Italian dish that is incredibly sumptuous, quick, and affordable to make. I enjoy the contrast in textures you get, that is, smooth white wine butter sauce, crispy prosciutto, and juicy chicken. Saltimbocca is typically made with veal, although it also tastes great when made with chicken, pork, or beef. Here, I make it with chicken as a cheaper and easily accessible option.

 PREPARATION TIME: **10 MINUTES** | COOKING TIME: **12 MINUTES**

SERVING SIZE: **2** | PER SERVING: **KCAL: 472; FAT: 20G; CARBS: 4G; PROTEIN: 66G; SUGARS: 2G; FIBRE: 2G**

Ingredients:

- 2 small chicken breast fillets
- Salt and black pepper to taste
- 4 fresh sage leaves
- 2 prosciutto slices
- 1 bunch thick asparagus spears, hard stems snipped off
- Extra virgin olive oil for coating
- Hollandaise sauce for serving
- Lemon wedges for serving

Instructions:

Step 1: Preheat the air fryer to 180°C.

Step 2: Season the chicken with salt and black pepper. On each chicken, place two sage leaves and then wrap each with one prosciutto.

Step 3: Place the wrapped chicken in the air fryer and cook for 8 minutes. After, coat the asparagus with a little oil and arrange them by the chicken. Cook for 4 minutes or until the chicken reaches an internal temperature of 74°C and the asparagus are tender.

Step 4: Plate the chicken and asparagus and serve warm with hollandaise sauce and lemon wedges.

HONEY BBQ CHICKEN WINGS

These chicken wings are flavourful, juicy, and tender. Generously seasoned, cooked until deliciously crispy, and then doused with a mouth-watering honey BBQ sauce, you'll be completely sold. They have a crunchy outside and a sweet, sticky touch. This recipe is the ideal appetiser for any occasion.

 PREPARATION TIME: **10 MINUTES** | COOKING TIME: **20 MINUTES**

 SERVING SIZE: **2** | PER SERVING: **KCAL: 226; FAT: 10G; CARBS: 21G; PROTEIN: 22G; SUGARS: 20G; FIBRE: 0G**

Ingredients:

- 200g chicken wings, joints separated
- 1 tbsp. olive oil
- Salt and black pepper to taste
- 2 tbsp. honey
- 1 tbsp. BBQ sauce
- Chopped fresh scallions for garnish

Instructions:

Step 1: Preheat the air fryer to 200°C.

Step 2: Season the chicken wings with olive oil, salt, and black pepper.

Step 3: Place the chicken in the air fryer in a single layer and air fry for 15 minutes or until golden while turning halfway through cooking.

Step 4: Meanwhile, in a large bowl, mix the honey and BBQ sauce. Remove the chicken into the bowl when ready and toss well.

Step 5: Line the air fryer with foil or parchment paper and arrange the coated chicken in it. Cook for 3 to 5 more minutes or until the sauce is sticky on the chicken.

Step 6: Remove the chicken onto a plate and garnish with scallions.

Step 7: Serve warm.

SHRIMP PO'BOYS

You'll be blown away by this real New Orleans shrimp po' boy with creamy sauce! Simple ingredients tweaked to English style but awesomely delicious.

 PREPARATION TIME: **15 MINUTES** | COOKING TIME: **8 MINUTES**

SERVING SIZE: **2** | PER SERVING: **KCAL: 1488; FAT: 56G; CARBS: 177G; PROTEIN: 69G; SUGARS: 45G; FIBRE: 9G**

Ingredients:

For the remoulade:

- 4 tbsp. mayonnaise
- 1 tbsp. English mustard
- 1 tbsp. finely chopped dill pickles or cornichons
- 1 tbsp. minced shallots
- 2 tbsp. fresh lemon juice
- ¼ tsp. cayenne pepper or to taste

For the shrimp:

- 250g plain flour
- 1 tsp. herbes de Provence
- 1 tsp. sea salt or to taste
- ½ tsp. garlic powder
- ½ tsp. black pepper
- ¼ tsp. cayenne pepper
- 1 large egg
- 250 ml semi-skimmed milk
- 1 tsp. hot sauce
- 400g raw shrimp, peeled and deveined
- Cooking oil

To assemble:

- 4 sub rolls, split
- 250g lettuce, shredded
- 1 medium tomato, thinly sliced

Instructions:

Step 1: Preheat the air fryer to 180°C.

For the remoulade:

Step 2: Mix the remoulade ingredients in a bowl and place them in the fridge to chill.

For the shrimp:

Step 3: On a plate, mix the flour, herbes de Provence, salt, garlic powder, black pepper, and cayenne pepper. Crack the egg into a bowl and whisk with the milk and hot sauce.

Step 4: Dip the shrimp in the eggs and coat well in the flour mixture.

Step 5: Brush the air fryer basket with a little cooking oil and arrange the shrimp in it in a single layer. Air fry for 3 to 4 minutes per side or until golden.

To assemble:

Step 6: In each sub roll, spread the lettuce and followed by the tomato slices. Add the shrimp and spread remoulade on the shrimp.

Step 7: Close the rolls and serve warm.

SHRIMP SCAMPI

Shrimp scampi is a great meal for week days. I make it often. It only requires a small number of ingredients, many of which you probably already have at home, and comes together quickly. For this seafood dish, shrimp are cooked in butter, and garlic sauce and then served with spaghetti. You can also serve it as a stand-alone appetiser.

 PREPARATION TIME: **10 MINUTES** | COOKING TIME: **12 MINUTES**

SERVING SIZE: **2** | PER SERVING: **KCAL: 263; FAT: 19G; CARBS: 3G; PROTEIN: 21G; SUGARS: 0G; FIBRE: 1G**

Ingredients:

- 200g raw shrimp, peeled and deveined with tails
- 2 garlic cloves, sliced
- 1 dried bay leaf
- Salt and black pepper to taste
- 1 tbsp. extra virgin olive oil
- 2 tbsp. unsalted butter
- 4 tbsp. flat-leaf parsley, finely chopped

Instructions:

Step 1: Preheat the air fryer to 180°C.

Step 2: In a small cooking pan (for the air fryer), combine all the ingredients except for the parsley. Cover the pan with foil.

Step 3: Place the pan in the air fryer and cook for 10 to 12 minutes or until the shrimp is pink and opaque.

Step 4: Take out and uncover the pan. Stir in the parsley and adjust the taste with salt and black pepper if needed.

Step 5: Serve the shrimp scampi with pasta.

BURRATA BOMB

For the love of extra cheesiness, we won't say no to this recipe. Even for brunch with all its gooey cheesiness and some pesto, this burrata bomb will please you any day. You'll never view burrata the same way anymore. This mild and creamy cheese is wrapped in pizza dough and air-fried as a whole.

 PREPARATION TIME: **10 MINUTES** | COOKING TIME: **12 MINUTES**

 SERVING SIZE: **2** | PER SERVING: **KCAL: 643; FAT: 39G; CARBS: 42G; PROTEIN: 32G; SUGARS: 5G; FIBRE: 1G**

Ingredients:

- Plain flour for dusting
- 1 small pizza dough, store-bought
- 1 tbsp. sun-dried tomato pesto
- 1 burrata ball
- 1 tsp. fresh basil leaves
- 1 tbsp. melted salted butter

Instructions:

Step 1: Preheat the air fryer to 170°C.

Step 2: Dust a clean, flat surface with flour and roll out the dough on it.

Step 3: Spread the pesto on the dough leaving a 6-8 cm border along the edges of the dough.

Step 4: Place the burrata ball at the centre of the pesto and top with the basil leaves. Wrap the dough over the burrata ball and twist the top to form a parcel. After, brush the dough with the butter.

Step 5: Sit the dough in the air fryer basket and bake for 10 to 12 minutes or until the dough is golden and crispy.

Step 6: Remove the burrata bomb and let it rest for a few minutes.

Step 7: Serve warm.

SOY SALMON WITH BROCCOLI

This Asian baked salmon is divine. The salmon is soft, moist, and not at all overcooked. The broccoli is also delightfully crisp and juicy from the sauce. It is a tasty combo perfect for lunches with family and friends.

PREPARATION TIME: 10 MINUTES | **COOKING TIME: 12 MINUTES**

SERVING SIZE: 2 | PER SERVING: **KCAL: 528; FAT: 22G; CARBS: 11G; PROTEIN: 69G; SUGARS: 4G; FIBRE: 4G**

Ingredients:

- 250g tiny broccoli florets
- 1 tbsp. vegetable oil
- Salt and black pepper to taste
- 1 tsp. soy sauce
- 1 tsp. light brown sugar
- 1 tbsp. rice vinegar
- A pinch of corn flour
- 1 cm piece ginger, peeled and grated
- 2 salmon fillets, skin on
- Sesame seeds for garnish

Instructions:

Step 1: Preheat the air fryer to 180°C.

Step 2: In a bowl, toss the broccoli with oil, salt, and black pepper. Put the broccoli in the air fryer while creating space for the salmon.

Step 3: In a small bowl, mix the soy sauce, brown sugar, rice vinegar, corn flour, and ginger. Brush the seasoning on the salmon. Sit the salmon (skin side facing upwards) by the broccoli in the air fryer.

Step 4: Air fry for 10 to 12 minutes or until the salmon is flaky and the broccoli is tender with a bite.

Step 5: Plate the salmon and broccoli, garnish with sesame seeds, and serve warm with rice.

SWEET AND SOUR PORK

Sweet and sour pork is one of the most well-known Chinese dishes in the UK. Instead of ordering takeout, make your own sweet and sour pork. It is cheaper, gives you more quantity, and the marinade is fantastic. If you don't like pork, swap it for chicken or prawns.

PREPARATION TIME: **10 MINUTES** | COOKING TIME: **12 MINUTES**

SERVING SIZE: **2** | PER SERVING: **KCAL: 606; FAT: 5G; CARBS: 90G; PROTEIN: 49G; SUGARS: 85G; FIBRE: 1G**

Ingredients:

- 120g can crushed unsweetened pineapple, undrained
- 4 tbsp. apple cider vinegar
- 4 tbsp. granulated sugar
- 4 tbsp. dark brown sugar
- 4 tbsp. ketchup
- 1 tsp. soy sauce, low-sodium
- 1 tbsp. Dijon mustard
- ½ tsp. garlic powder
- 450g pork tenderloin, cut into 3 cm pieces
- Salt and black pepper to taste
- Sliced green onions for garnish

Instructions:

Step 1: In a saucepan, combine all the ingredients except for the pork, salt, black pepper, and green onions. Simmer the sauce over medium heat (on a stovetop) for 6 to 8 minutes or until thickened while stirring occasionally.

Step 2: Preheat the air fryer to 180°C.

Step 3: Season the pork with salt and black pepper. Place it in the air fryer basket in a single layer and cook for 10 to 12 minutes or until golden and reaches an internal temperature of 63°C.

Step 4: Transfer the pork to the sweet and sour sauce and warm over low heat on the stove top for 1 to 2 minutes.

Step 5: Garnish with green onions and serve with rice.

SWEET AND SPICY MEATBALLS

Do you have a weekend favourite food? If not, then let these sweet and spicy meatballs be it. They are all that your pasta or sub sandwiches need. They are a little bit sweet, a little bit savoury, and somewhat spicy. Serve them as football appetisers too.

PREPARATION TIME: **15 MINUTES** | COOKING TIME: **17 MINUTES**

SERVING SIZE: **2** | PER SERVING: **KCAL: 1497; FAT: 36G; CARBS: 222G; PROTEIN: 77G; SUGARS: 112G; FIBRE: 13G**

Ingredients:

For the meatballs:

- 150g quick-cooking oats
- 140g crushed Ritz crackers
- 2 large eggs, lightly beaten
- 4 tbsp. evaporated milk
- 1 tsp. chopped dried onion
- 2 tsp. salt
- 2 tsp. garlic powder
- 1 tsp. ground cumin
- ½ tsp. black pepper
- 2 tsp. honey
- 450g 90% lean beef mince
- Cooking oil for coating

For the sauce:

- 80g brown sugar
- 4 tbsp. honey
- 4 tbsp. marmalade
- 2 tbsp. corn flour
- 4 tbsp. soy sauce
- 2 tbsp. hot sauce
- 1 tbsp. Worcestershire sauce

Instructions:

Step 1: Preheat the air fryer to 190°C.

For the meatballs:
Step 2: Add all the meatball ingredients to a bowl and mix well. Form 3-cm-sized balls from the mixture.

Step 3: Coat the meatballs with a little oil and place them in the air fryer. Air fry them for 12 to 15 minutes or until they are nicely browned, turning them halfway through cooking.

For the sauce:
Step 4: Meanwhile, in a small pot, combine the sauce's ingredients and cook over low heat for 4 to 5 minutes or until thickened.

Step 5: Brush the meatballs with the sauce and cook for 2 more minutes.

Step 6: Plate the meatballs and serve them over pasta, in sandwiches, vegetables, etc.

TAQUITO AND CHARRED SALSA

These warm, cheesy, and very crispy wrapped tacos called taquitos are your perfect easy lunch treat. Serve them with warm charred salsa on a lazy day and enjoy the chill. Right from Mexico to you, they burst out ooey gooey cheese with other chunky fillings. Once you master making them, you can load up the fillings as you like; I love some chicken in there.

⏱ PREPARATION TIME: **10 MINUTES** | 🍲 COOKING TIME: **8 MINUTES**

🛎 SERVING SIZE: **2** | PER SERVING: **KCAL: 1,407; FAT: 68G; CARBS: 123G; PROTEIN: 76G; SUGARS: 9G; FIBRE: 10G**

Ingredients:

For the charred salsa:

- 250g Roma tomatoes
- 1 small onion, peeled and cut into eight wedges
- 1 serrano pepper, stems intact
- 1 garlic clove, peeled
- 1 tbsp. extra virgin olive oil
- Salt to taste

Taquitos:

- 300g rotisserie chicken, chopped
- 120g grated Mexican-style chilli cheddar cheese
- 120g diced pimientos, drained
- 1 tsp. dried oregano
- ½ tsp. cumin powder
- ½ tsp. paprika
- ½ tsp. chilli powder
- Salt to taste
- 1 pack of small maize tortillas
- 120g refried beans
- Soured cream for serving
- Romaine lettuce, shredded for serving

Instructions:

Step 1: Preheat the air fryer to 180°C.

For the charred salsa:

Step 2: In a bowl, toss the tomatoes, onion, serrano pepper, and garlic with oil and salt. Spread the mixture in the air fryer basket and roast for 10 minutes or until the tomatoes are slightly blackened.

Step 3: Remove the vegetables onto a plate and let cool to touch. Peel the tomatoes' skin and remove the pepper's stem and seeds. After, blend the vegetables until smooth to your desire. Set aside for serving.

For the taquitos:

Step 4: In a bowl, mix all the ingredients except for the tortillas, refried beans, soured cream, and romaine lettuce.

Step 5: Lay out the tortillas separately and spread 2 teaspoons of refried beans on top to the edges. After, add 1½ tbsp. of chicken mixture on top leaving a bit of the edges for sealing. Tightly roll the tortillas over the filling, not too tight to break the tortillas, however.

Step 6: Mist the tortillas with cooking spray and place them in the air fryer basket with the sealed sides facing downwards. Air fry for 8 minutes or until golden and crispy.

Step 7: Transfer them to a plate and top with the charred salsa and soured cream. Serve with lettuce shreds.

TOSTONES WITH CREAMY MOJO DIPPING SAUCE

Tostones are technically made with green plantains but I love mine sweet, so I use nearly ripe plantains for this recipe. Paired with mojo dipping sauce that is a citrus-garlic-herb sauce, there's much to love here. Call this a light lunch when you just need a quick refill. The air fryer fries the plantains to perfection, so you get a lovely crunch with all that natural sweetness.

 PREPARATION TIME: **10 MINUTES** | COOKING TIME: **13 MINUTES**

 SERVING SIZE: **2** | PER SERVING: **KCAL: 821; FAT: 35G; CARBS: 117G; PROTEIN: 22G; SUGARS: 67G; FIBRE: 7G**

Ingredients:

- 2 medium nearly ripe green plantains, peeled
- 200 ml warm water
- ½ tsp. rock salt, plus more to taste
- ½ tsp. plus 1 pinch of garlic powder
- 1 tbsp. finely chopped fresh coriander
- 3 tbsp. plain full-fat Greek yoghurt
- 1 tbsp. olive oil
- 1 tbsp. fresh lime juice
- 1 tbsp. fresh orange juice
- ½ tsp. ground cumin

Instructions:

Step 1: Preheat the air fryer to 200°C.

Step 2: Cut the plantains into 3 cm slices and coat them with a little cooking oil.

Step 3: Place them in the air fryer basket and fry for 6 minutes or until they are soft enough to be crushed.

Step 4: Remove the plantains onto a chopping board and use the bottom of a glass cup to crush each slice into a disc.

Step 5: In a bowl, combine the warm water, salt, and garlic powder. Whisk until the salt dissolves. Put the tostones in the water and let them soak for 5 minutes. Remove them after and dry them with paper towels. Mist them with cooking spray.

Step 6: Place them in the air fryer basket and fry them for 7 more minutes or until they are golden and crisp. Season them with salt.

Step 7: In a bowl, mix the Greek yoghurt, olive oil, lime juice, and orange juice until smooth.

Step 8: Serve the tostones with sauce.

SCAN ME

Please scan the QR code below to access your bonus PDF with all 150 recipes with full coloured photos & beautiful designs alongside! This is the only way we can get the recipes with coloured photos to you & keep the book as reasonably priced as possible.

Also, once downloaded you can take the PDF with you digitally wherever you go- meaning you can cook these recipes wherever you may be! (As long as you have an air fryer!)

We hope you enjoy and do let us know your feedback!

STEP BY STEP GUIDE TO ACCESS

1. Open Your Phones (Or Any Device You Want The Book On) Back Camera. The Back Camera Is The One You use as if you are taking a picture of someone.
2. Simply point your Camera at the QR code and 'tap' the QR code with your finger to focus the camera.
3. A link / pop up will appear. Simply tap that (and make sure you have internet connection) and the FREE PDF containing all of the coloured images should appear.
4. Now you have access to these FOREVER. Simply 'Bookmark' The tab it opened on, or download the document and take wherever you want.
5. Repeat this on any device you want it on! (If you want it on a laptop, simply email the document to yourself!)

Any issues please email us at:
vicandersonpublishing@gmail.com
and we will be happy to help!!

Dinner Recipes

APRICOT-GLAZED CHICKEN BREASTS

Apricot preserves are awesome for coating chicken, giving it glazy stickiness and subtle tangy sweetness. This recipe is a quick pass for making sweet and sour chicken without much fuss.

⏱ PREPARATION TIME: **10 MINUTES** | 🍲 COOKING TIME: **10 MINUTES**

🍽 SERVING SIZE: **2** | PER SERVING: **KCAL: 531; FAT: 29G; CARBS: 3G; PROTEIN: 61G; SUGARS: 2; FIBRE: 0G**

Ingredients:

- 1 tsp. apricot jam
- 1 tsp. fresh ginger paste
- ½ tsp. freshly minced rosemary
- 2 (100g) chicken breasts, skinless and boneless
- 1 tsp. vegetable oil
- Salt and black pepper to taste

Instructions:

Step 1: Preheat the air fryer to 200°C.

Step 2: In a bowl, mix the apricot jam, ginger paste, and rosemary.

Step 3: Brush the chicken with vegetable oil and season with salt and black pepper.

Step 4: Place the chicken in the air fryer and bake for 4 minutes per side.

Step 5: Brush the chicken with the apricot sauce and cook for 2 more minutes or until the chicken is sticky or until it reaches an internal temperature of 73°C.

Step 6: Transfer the chicken to a plate and let it rest for 5 minutes.

Step 7: Serve warm.

· ·

BALSAMIC PORK CHOPS

Balsamic pork chops are great midweek meals. They are slightly sweet, acidic, and sitting beneath their catchy brown coating, is a yummy golden crust. After being "grilled", these succulent, boneless pork chops are covered in a delectable honey balsamic sauce. A little raspberry jam goes in for a sticky texture and to enhance its sweet taste.

⏱ PREPARATION TIME: **10 MINUTES** | 🍲 COOKING TIME: **13 MINUTES**

🍽 SERVING SIZE: **2** | PER SERVING: **KCAL: 365; FAT: 9G; CARBS: 27G; PROTEIN: 42G; SUGARS: 25G; FIBRE: 0G**

Ingredients:

- Cooking oil
- 2 boneless pork chops
- Salt and black pepper to taste
- 4 tbsp. balsamic vinegar
- 2 tbsp. honey
- 2 tsp. raspberry jam without seeds
- 5g defrosted frozen orange juice concentrate

Instructions:

Step 1: Preheat the air fryer to 200°C.

Step 2: Brush the pork chops with oil and season with salt and black pepper.

Step 3: Place the pork chops in the air fryer and cook for 4 to 5 minutes per side or until golden and reaches an internal temperature of 64°C.

Step 4: In a bowl, mix the balsamic vinegar, honey, raspberry jam, and orange juice concentrate.

Step 5: Brush the pork chops with the balsamic mixture. Cook for 2 to 3 more minutes or until sticky.

Step 6: Remove the pork from the air fryer and let it rest for 5 to 10 minutes.

Step 7: Serve warm.

BEEF MINCE WELLINGTON

Are you looking to host friends over soon? Beef Wellington is perfect for them. Slice through the excellently crusted pastry into properly cooked beef as an awesome reveal to your friends. Making Beef Wellington is a journey in itself. In this traditional British dish, beef mince is moulded into tenderloin and then wrapped in layers of buttery puff pastry. After, it is baked to a golden, flaky outside, and juicy done inside.

 PREPARATION TIME: **15 MINUTES** | COOKING TIME: **36 MINUTES**

SERVING SIZE: **2** | PER SERVING: **KCAL: 748; FAT: 53G; CARBS: 27G; PROTEIN: 42G; SUGARS: 9G; FIBRE: 3G**

Ingredients:

- 2 tsp. butter
- 4 tbsp. freshly sliced mushrooms
- 2 tsp. plain flour
- ½ tsp. black pepper or to taste
- 150 ml single cream
- 1 large egg yolk
- 2 tsp. onion, finely chopped
- 250g beef mince
- 1 tsp. salt or to taste
- 4 prosciutto slices
- 1 pack of chilled croissant dough
- 1 large egg, lightly beaten

Instructions:

Step 1: Preheat the air fryer to 160°C.

Step 2: Melt the butter in a skillet over medium heat and sauté the mushrooms for 8 minutes or until the liquid has evaporated and they are tender. Stir in the flour and season with black pepper. Cook for 1 minute and then stir in the cream. Simmer for 4 to 5 minutes and turn the heat off. Set aside. (You can also do this while the beef bakes but I prefer to make it earlier for the flavours to combine well over time).

Step 3: In a bowl, whisk the egg yolk, onion, beef, and salt until well combined. Form the beef mixture into two loaves and wrap each with two prosciutto slices.

Step 4: Roll the dough and form into 2 rectangles; seal the perforations. Place one wrapped meat at the centre of one dough rectangle. After, wrap them over the meat and brush their tops with egg.

Step 5: Coat the air fryer with a little cooking spray and place the beef pastry in the air fryer. Bake for 18 to 22 minutes or until golden brown and the beef reaches an internal temperature of 64°C.

Step 6: Take them out of the air fryer and let rest for 5 to 10 minutes before slicing.

Step 7: Reheat the mushroom sauce and serve with the Beef Wellington.

CHICKEN KATSU WITH HOMEMADE KATSU SAUCE

Golden and crispy, and bathed over with a sweet tangy sauce, this chicken katsu is made to improve your dinner options. It is perfectly and easily made in the air fryer. Serve it with rice for a fuller meal.

⏱ PREPARATION TIME: **10 MINUTES** | 🍲 COOKING TIME: **15 MINUTES**

🍽 SERVING SIZE: **2** | PER SERVING: **CAL: 657; FAT: 13G; CARBS: 93G; PROTEIN: 41G; SUGARS: 22G; FIBRE: 5G**

Ingredients:

For the katsu sauce:

- 100 ml ketchup
- 2 tsp. soy sauce
- 2 tsp. brown sugar
- 1 tbsp. sherry vinegar
- 2 tbsp. Worcestershire sauce
- 1 tsp. garlic mince

For the chicken:

- 200g boneless and skinless chicken breasts, sliced
- Salt and black pepper to taste
- 2 large eggs, beaten
- 200g panko breadcrumbs

Instructions:

Step 1: Preheat the air fryer to 175°C.

Step 2: In a small pot, combine the sauce's ingredients and mix until the sugar dissolves. Cook the sauce over medium heat for 4 to 5 minutes or until thickened. Set aside.

Step 3: Season the chicken with salt and black pepper. Dip the chicken in the eggs and coat well with the breadcrumbs. After, mist the chicken on both sides with cooking spray.

Step 4: Place the chicken in the air fryer and cook for 4 to 5 minutes per side or until golden and the chicken reaches an internal temperature of 73°C.

Step 5: Transfer the chicken to a platter when ready and drizzle on the katsu sauce. Let rest for 5 minutes and serve warm.

CRUMB-TOPPED SOLE

These sole fillets are juicy and soak up much flavour. The attractive, golden crusting makes them ideal for weekend nights. They melt on your tongue, making it a tasty weeknight meal. It is simple, delicious, and pairs with many sauces.

PREPARATION TIME: **10 MINUTES** | COOKING TIME: **11 MINUTES**

SERVING SIZE: **2** | PER SERVING: **KCAL: 593; FAT: 31G; CARBS: 46G; PROTEIN: 31G; SUGARS: 4G; FIBRE: 3G**

Ingredients:

- 3 tbsp. low-fat mayonnaise
- 3 tbsp. grated Parmesan cheese
- 2 tsp. mustard seeds
- 1 tbsp, black pepper or to taste
- 2 sole fillets
- Salt to taste
- 120g tender breadcrumbs
- ½ tsp. ground mustard
- 2 tsp. melted butter
- Cooking oil

Instructions:

Step 1: Preheat the air fryer to 180°C.

Step 2: In a small bowl, mix the mayonnaise, Parmesan cheese, mustard seeds, and black pepper.

Step 3: Season the fish with salt and brush their tops with the mustard mixture.

Step 4: Coat the air fryer basket with a little cooking oil and lay the fish in it. Cook for 6 to 8 minutes.

Step 5: Meanwhile, in a bowl, mix the breadcrumbs, mustard, and butter. Spoon the mixture on the fish and cook for 2 to 3 more minutes or until golden brown.

Step 6: Remove the fish onto a plate and serve warm.

DIJON-MAPLE GLAZED SALMON

This 15-minute Dijon-Maple Glazed Salmon is a low-calorie, high-protein supper. The fish's interior bakes to delicate perfection as the tangy-sweet sauce caramelises the exterior. Have you ever had salmon that is so soft and flaky that it almost melts in your mouth? If not, this ridiculously easy recipe will get you there in no time.

PREPARATION TIME: **5 MINUTES** | COOKING TIME: **9 MINUTES**

SERVING SIZE: **2** | PER SERVING: **KCAL: 556; FAT: 27G; CARBS: 10G; PROTEIN: 66G; SUGARS: 7G; FIBRE: 1G**

Ingredients:

- 2 salmon fillets
- 1 tbsp. olive oil
- Salt and black pepper to taste
- 1 tbsp. butter, melted
- 1 tbsp. maple syrup
- 1 tbsp. Dijon mustard
- 1 small lemon, juiced
- 1 tsp. garlic powder

Instructions:

Step 1: Preheat the air fryer to 200°C.

Step 2: Brush the salmon with olive oil and season with salt and black pepper.

Step 3: Place the salmon in the air fryer and bake for 5 to 6 minutes.

Step 4: Meanwhile, in a bowl, mix the remaining ingredients until smooth. When the air fryer's timer is off, brush the sauce on the salmon. Cook the salmon for 2 to 3 more minutes or until golden and flaky.

Step 5: Plate the salmon and serve warm.

FRIED RICE WITH SESAME-SRIRACHA SAUCE

A low-budget meal that is comfy and easy to make. Here, I show you a simple way to cook fried rice and pair it with spicy sesame sauce for good measure. With a little tweak, you can make the best fried rice you ever had. The rice isn't soggy as skillet cooking sometimes is because the air fryer dries out the extra moisture. All you need are some day-old cooked white rice and a couple of vegetables. Let's start!

⏱ PREPARATION TIME: **10 MINUTES** | 🍲 COOKING TIME: **8 MINUTES**

🍽 SERVING SIZE: **2** | PER SERVING: **KCAL: 528; FAT: 18G; CARBS: 79G; PROTEIN: 13G; SUGARS: 6G; FIBRE: 8G**

Ingredients:

- 400g cooked white rice, day-old
- 1 tbsp. vegetable oil
- 1 tbsp. toasted sesame oil
- 1 tsp. water
- Salt and black pepper to taste
- Sriracha sauce to taste
- 1 tsp. soy sauce
- One egg, lightly beaten
- 250g frozen peas, thawed
- 250g diced carrots
- Sesame seeds for garnish

Instructions:

Step 1: Preheat the air fryer to 200°C.

Step 2: In a cooking pan (for the air fryer), mix the rice, oil, half of the sesame oil, water, salt, and black pepper.

Step 3: Meanwhile, in a bowl, mix the remaining sesame oil, sriracha, and soy sauce. Cook for 2 more minutes.

Step 4: Pour the egg over the rice, mix well and cook for 4 minutes or until the egg sets.

Step 5: Add the peas and carrots, and cook for 2 more minutes or until they are warm and tender. Adjust the fried rice's taste with salt and black pepper if needed.

Step 6: Spoon the fried rice into serving bowls and garnish with sesame seeds. Serve warm.

HERB-CRUSTED SALMON WITH POTATOES

Such a no-fuss dinner that still carries some character. Enjoy an aromatic herb crusting over salmon with well flaky insides. No better way to serve this salmon than with potatoes. A party-worthy fish dinner that oozes lemon herb aromas and then served with fluffy baby potatoes.

PREPARATION TIME: **10 MINUTES** | COOKING TIME: **10 MINUTES**

SERVING SIZE: **2** | PER SERVING: **KCAL: 653; FAT: 28G; CARBS: 28G; PROTEIN: 69G; SUGARS: 2G; FIBRE: 3G**

Ingredients:

- 250g quartered kestrel potatoes, peeled and cut into wedges
- 1 tsp. olive oil
- Salt and black pepper to taste
- 1 slice of day-old bread
- 2 tbsp. melted butter + extra for brushing
- 1 tsp. chopped fresh dill, plus additional for garnish
- 1 tsp. chopped fresh chives
- 2 (180g) salmon fillets
- Lemon wedges for serving

Instructions:

Step 1: Preheat the air fryer to 180°C.

Step 2: In a bowl, toss the potatoes with olive oil, salt, and black pepper. Put the potatoes in the air fryer and roast for 20 minutes or until golden and fork tender.

Step 3: Meanwhile, in a food processor, crumble the bread. Add the butter, dill, chives, salt, and black pepper and blitz a few times to combine.

Step 4: Brush the salmon with a little butter and spread the herb breading on the flesh.

Step 5: When the potatoes are ready, transfer them to a plate and place the salmon in the air fryer with the skin side facing downwards. Bake the salmon for 8 to 10 minutes or until the crust is golden and the salmon is flaky.

Step 6: Remove the salmon onto serving plates and serve with the potatoes.

INSIDE-OUTSIDE VEGETABLE LASAGNE

Ricotta cheese, pasta, and tomatoes, let's talk lasagne. However, here there's no layering. It cuts out the prep and cooking time for a remarkably quick and filling supper for the entire family. Separately cook the different layers of traditional lasagne and then serve them together in bowls. It's that easy!

PREPARATION TIME: 10 MINUTES | **COOKING TIME: 10 MINUTES**

SERVING SIZE: 2 | PER SERVING: **KCAL: 243; FAT: 12G; CARBS: 27G; PROTEIN: 12G; SUGARS: 5G; FIBRE: 6G**

Ingredients:

- 100g whole wheat fusilli or rotini
- 1 tbsp. extra virgin olive oil
- 1 onion, sliced
- 4 tbsp. thinly sliced white mushrooms
- 1 tbsp. minced garlic
- Salt and black pepper to taste
- 4 tbsp. chopped tomatoes with Italian seasoning
- 250g baby spinach
- ½ tsp. red pepper flakes (optional)
- 4 tbsp. ricotta cheese

Instructions:

Step 1: Preheat the air fryer to 150°C.

Step 2: Cook the pasta according to the package's instructions. Drain and set aside.

Step 3: Meanwhile, in an air fryer cooking pan, add the olive oil, onion, and mushrooms. Place the pan in the air fryer and cook for 5 minutes. Stir in the garlic and cook for 1 minute. Season with salt and black pepper.

Step 4: Pour in the tomatoes, spinach, and red pepper flakes (if using). Cook for 4 minutes while stirring halfway. Adjust the taste with salt and black pepper if needed.

Step 5: Divide the pasta into serving bowls and top with the tomato sauce. Add ricotta cheese and serve warm.

MUSTARD-CRUSTED PORK TENDERLOIN WITH POTATOES AND GREEN BEANS

Such an irresistible dish, pork tenderloin with delicious mustard crusting pairs with potatoes and green beans. A fantastic meal to enjoy with a loved one. It is a simple yet satisfying combo that will leave you joyful. Mustard lends in some tang to the pork and authenticates its savouriness.

PREPARATION TIME: **10 MINUTES** | COOKING TIME: **35 MINUTES**

SERVING SIZE: **2** | PER SERVING: **KCAL: 223; FAT: 5G; CARBS: 21G; PROTEIN: 24G; SUGARS: 8G; FIBRE: 4G**

Ingredients:

- 1 tbsp. Dijon mustard
- 1 tbsp. brown sugar
- 1 tsp. dried parsley flakes
- ½ tsp. dried thyme
- Salt and black pepper to taste
- Olive oil for coating
- 200g pork tenderloin
- 100g small potatoes
- 200g fresh green beans

Instructions:

Step 1: Preheat the air fryer to 200°C.

Step 2: In a bowl, mix the mustard, brown sugar, parsley, thyme, salt, and black pepper. Press the mixture all over the pork.

Step 3: Coat the air fryer basket with cooking oil and sit the pork in it. Cook the pork for 20 minutes without flipping it until it is nicely browned and reaches an internal temperature of 64°C.

Step 4: Remove the pork onto a chopping board and let rest for 10 to 15 minutes.

Step 5: Meanwhile, coat the potatoes and green beans with olive oil and season with salt and black pepper. Put the potatoes in the air fryer and cook for 10 to 12 minutes or until the potatoes are almost fork tender. Add the green beans and cook for 3 minutes or until they are tender with a bite and the potatoes are cooked.

Step 6: Slice the pork and serve with the ready potatoes and green beans.

PARMESAN-CRUSTED CHICKEN WITH BROCCOLI

Thanks to a little breadcrumb and Parmesan crusting and a fast air fryer cook, this chicken dish becomes wonderfully crispy! It is a balanced and healthy dinner that you can prepare several times a week. Serve it with browned broccoli and tart yoghurt sauce.

⏱ PREPARATION TIME: **10 MINUTES** | 🍲 COOKING TIME: **12 MINUTES**

🍽 SERVING SIZE: **2** | PER SERVING: **KCAL: 725; FAT: 34G; CARBS: 31G; PROTEIN: 74G; SUGARS: 8G; FIBRE: 8G**

Ingredients:

- 4 tbsp. panko breadcrumbs
- 4 tbsp. finely grated Parmesan
- ½ tsp. dried oregano
- Salt and black pepper to taste
- 2 chicken breasts, skinless and boneless
- 2 tsp. English mustard
- Olive oil for coating
- 500g tiny broccoli florets
- 4 tbsp. plain low-fat yoghurt
- ½ lemon, zested and juiced

Instructions:

Step 1: Preheat the air fryer to 180°C.

Step 2: In a bowl, mix the breadcrumbs, Parmesan, oregano, salt, and black pepper. Brush the chicken with mustard and coat with the Parmesan mixture.

Step 3: Coat the air fryer basket with a little olive oil and place the chicken in it.

Step 4: Season the broccoli with olive oil, salt, and black pepper and put it by the chicken. Cook for 10 to 12 minutes or until the chicken is golden and reaches an internal temperature of 73°C.

Step 5: Meanwhile, in a bowl, mix the yoghurt, lemon zest, and juice.

Step 6: Plate the chicken and broccoli. Let the chicken rest for 5 minutes.

Step 7: Serve warm with the tart yoghurt sauce.

PASTA TACOS

Until I tried these tacos in large pasta shells, I didn't know what I was missing. Since the air fryer makes them so effortlessly and excellently, they are my go-to dinner option when I want a light splurge. Cook up the taco meat and then stuff it in large pasta shells. After, bake them with some cheese and you have a rich dish.

PREPARATION TIME: **10 MINUTES** | COOKING TIME: **20 MINUTES**

SERVING SIZE: **2** | PER SERVING: **KCAL: 1454; FAT: 97G; CARBS: 81G; PROTEIN: 71G; SUGARS: 8G; FIBRE: 16G**

Ingredients:

- 14 large shells of pasta
- 1 tbsp. virgin extra olive oil
- 1 shallot, minced
- 90g beef mince
- 1 tsp. cumin powder
- 1 tsp. ground coriander
- 1 tsp. garlic powder
- Salt and black pepper to taste
- 100 ml jar thick and chunky salsa
- 4 tbsp. black beans
- 1 tsp. chilli powder
- 3 tbsp. grated cheddar cheese
- 2 tomatoes, diced
- 1 avocado, pitted, peeled, and diced

To serve:

- Fresh coriander sprigs
- Soured cream
- Lime wedges

Instructions:

Step 1: Preheat the air fryer to 150°C.

Step 2: Cook the pasta shells according to the package's instructions. Drain and set them aside.

Step 3: Meanwhile, in a skillet, heat the olive oil over medium heat and sauté the shallot for 2 minutes. Add the beef and cook for 8 minutes while breaking the meat with your spoon. Season with the cumin powder, coriander, garlic powder, salt, and black pepper. Cook for 2 more minutes.

Step 4: Pour in the salsa, black beans, and chilli powder. Stir well.

Step 5: Spoon the meat mixture into the pasta shells and top them with the cheddar cheese.

Step 6: Lightly coat the air fryer basket with cooking oil and sit the pasta shells in it. Bake for 5 to 8 minutes or until the pasta shells are golden and the cheese melted.

Step 7: Plate them and top them with the diced tomatoes and avocado.

Step 8: Serve warm with coriander, soured cream, and lime wedges.

PRETZEL CATFISH

I find pretzels to be a good tasting snack that crusts fish so well. So, let's pick out some honey mustard ones, crush them, and crust some fish. You may have chanced upon on the best crusted fish yet that has a completely new taste different from breadcrumb crusting. Pretzels to the rescue!

⏱ PREPARATION TIME: **10 MINUTES** | 🍲 COOKING TIME: **10 MINUTES**

🍽 SERVING SIZE: **2** | PER SERVING: **KCAL: 678; FAT: 12G; CARBS: 99G; PROTEIN: 42G; SUGARS: 1G; FIBRE: 3G**

Ingredients:

- 2 catfish fillets
- Salt and black pepper to taste
- 1 large egg
- 1 tbsp. English mustard
- 1 tbsp. semi-skimmed milk
- 4 tbsp. plain flour
- 900g small honey mustard pretzels, crushed
- Cooking oil for coating
- Lemon slices for serving, if desired

Instructions:

Step 1: Preheat the air fryer to 180°C.

Step 2: Season the catfish with salt and black pepper.

Step 3: Crack the egg into a bowl and whisk with mustard and milk. Spread the flour on a plate and crushed pretzels on another.

Step 4: Dredge the fish in flour, dip in the egg mixture, and coat well with the pretzels.

Step 5: Lightly grease the air fryer basket with cooking oil and lay the fish in it. Bake for 8 to 10 minutes or until golden and the fish is flaky.

Step 6: Plate the fish and serve with the lemon slices.

· ·

TORTELLINI AI FORMAGGI WITH PROSCIUTTO

When I crave a simple yet delicious dish that can be made quickly without any mess, this pasta recipe is my go-to dinner. Tortellini ai formaggi with prosciutto is a delightful and simple dish to cook. It is a special, simple, and quick dinner for you and your significant other.

⏱ PREPARATION TIME: **10 MINUTES** | 🍲 COOKING TIME: **5 MINUTES**

🍽 SERVING SIZE: **2** | PER SERVING: **KCAL: 529; FAT: 15G; CARBS: 73G; PROTEIN: 25G; SUGARS: 2G; FIBRE: 3G**

Ingredients:

- 1 (300 g) packet chilled prosciutto and ricotta tortellini
- 1 large egg
- 2 tsp. semi-skimmed milk
- Salt and black pepper to taste
- 2 tsp. grated Pecorino Romano cheese
- 1 tsp. garlic powder
- Olive oil for coating
- 2 tsp. freshly minced parsley

Instructions:

Step 1: Preheat the air fryer to 160°C.

Step 2: Cook the tortellini according to the package's instructions.

Step 3: Crack the egg into a bowl and whisk with the milk, salt, and black pepper. On a plate, mix the cheese and garlic powder.

Step 4: Dip the tortellini in the egg mix and then coat well with the cheese mix.

Step 5: Line the air fryer basket with foil and arrange the tortellini in it. Bake for 4 to 5 minutes or until the cheese melts.

Step 6: Remove the tortellini onto a plate and serve with cheese or basil tomato sauce.

SALSA VERDE CHICKEN WITH LEMON KALE SALAD

This winning combination, that is, juicy chicken and zesty salsa verde kale salad, is ideal for a weekend dinner. Serve it with lightly buttered new potatoes for a tasty family meal!

⏱ PREPARATION TIME: **10 MINUTES** | 🍲 COOKING TIME: **12 MINUTES**

🍽 SERVING SIZE: **2** | PER SERVING: **KCAL: 951; FAT: 61G; CARBS: 50G; PROTEIN: 51G; SUGARS: 4G; FIBRE: 7G**

Ingredients:

For the chicken thighs:

- 2 chicken thighs, bone-in and skin-on
- 1 tsp. olive oil
- 2 tsp. lemon zest, finely grated
- Salt and black pepper to taste

For the salsa verde:

- 2 tsp. capers
- 100g anchovy fillets with oil (optional)
- 1 garlic clove
- Salt to taste
- 2 tbsp. olive oil
- 1 tsp. red wine vinegar
- 1 tsp. fresh lemon zest
- 1 tbsp. finely chopped fresh parsley
- 4 tbsp. finely chopped fresh basil leaves
- ½ small bunch chives, finely chopped

For the kale salad:

- 3 tsp. fresh lemon juice
- 1 tbsp. English mustard
- 1 tsp. fresh lemon zest
- 1 tsp. crushed red pepper flakes
- Salt and black pepper to taste
- 1 tbsp. olive oil
- 50g curly kale, stems removed and leaves thinly sliced
- 100g croutons
- 1 tbsp. finely grated Pecorino Romano, plus extra for serving

Instructions:

Step 1: Preheat the air fryer to 180°C.

For the chicken thighs:

Step 2: Coat the chicken with olive oil and season with lemon zest, salt, and black pepper.

Step 3: Place the chicken in the air fryer basket and cook for 4 to 6 minutes or until golden brown and reaches an internal temperature of 73°C.

For the salsa verde:

Step 4: While the chicken cooks, combine all the salsa verde ingredients in a blender and blend until smooth to your desire. Set aside for serving.

For the kale salad:

Step 5: In a bowl, whisk the olive oil, lemon juice, mustard, lemon zest, red pepper flakes, salt, and black pepper.

Step 6: In a bowl, combine the kale, croutons, and Pecorino Romano. Drizzle the dressing on top and toss well.

Step 7: When the chicken is ready, serve it with the kale salad and salsa verde.

STEAK WITH GARLIC HERB BUTTER

My family enjoys a wonderful steak dinner, and the one ingredient mix that elevates its flavour is butter with garlic and herbs. It effortlessly transforms an excellent cut of steak into a dish fit for a high-end restaurant. My simple steak butter recipe gives any beef dish, including beef mince burgers, steaks, and even Sunday roasts, a hit of flavour that always wins.

⏱ PREPARATION TIME: **10 MINUTES** | 🍲 COOKING TIME: **12 MINUTES**

🍽 SERVING SIZE: **2** | PER SERVING: **KCAL: 657; FAT: 50G; CARBS: 2G; PROTEIN: 47G; SUGARS: 1G; FIBRE: 0G**

Ingredients:

- 450g (3 cm) thick sirloin steak
- 1 tsp. olive oil
- Salt and black pepper to taste
- 4 tbsp. unsalted butter
- 2 tsp. chopped fresh parsley
- 2 tsp. chopped fresh chives
- 1 small garlic clove, minced
- ½ tsp. crushed red pepper flakes

Instructions:

Step 1: Preheat the air fryer to 200°C.

Step 2: Brush the beef with a little oil and season with salt and black pepper.

Step 3: Place the steak in the air fryer basket and cook for 8 to 12 minutes or until it reaches an internal temperature of 64°C.

Step 4: Meanwhile, in a bowl, mix the butter, parsley, chives, garlic, and red pepper flakes.

Step 5: When the steak is ready, plate them and spoon some of the garlic herb butter on top. Let them rest for 5 minutes before slicing and serving.

CHRISTMAS TURKEY

Your Christmas dinner could succeed or fail depending on the dryness of the turkey. Fortunately, cooking a perfectly moist and tasty turkey is not that difficult. This dish for Christmas turkey couldn't be more adored.

⏱ PREPARATION TIME: **10 MINUTES** | 🍲 COOKING TIME: **40 MINUTES**

🍽 SERVING SIZE: **2** | PER SERVING: **KCAL: 610; FAT: 28G; CARBS: 3G; PROTEIN: 82G; SUGARS: 1G; FIBRE: 1G**

Ingredients:

- 1 tsp. rock salt
- 1 tbsp. dried thyme
- 1 tsp. dried ground rosemary
- ½ tsp. black pepper
- ½ tsp. dried sage
- ½ tsp. garlic powder
- ½ tsp. paprika
- ½ tsp. dark brown sugar
- 900g whole turkey, well-cleaned
- Olive oil for brushing

Instructions:

Step 1: Preheat the air fryer to 170°C.

Step 2: In a bowl, mix all the ingredients except for the turkey and olive oil.

Step 3: Brush the turkey all around with olive oil and season every side with the spice mixture.

Step 4: Place the turkey in the air fryer and roast for 20 minutes. Turn the chicken and roast for 20 more minutes or until the breast reaches an internal temperature of 73°C.

Step 5: Remove the turkey onto a chopping board and let rest for 10 minutes.

Step 6: Slice the turkey and serve warm.

SCAN ME

Please scan the QR code below to access your bonus PDF with all 150 recipes with full coloured photos & beautiful designs alongside! This is the only way we can get the recipes with coloured photos to you & keep the book as reasonably priced as possible.

Also, once downloaded you can take the PDF with you digitally wherever you go- meaning you can cook these recipes wherever you may be! (As long as you have an air fryer!)

We hope you enjoy and do let us know your feedback!

STEP BY STEP GUIDE TO ACCESS

1. Open Your Phones (Or Any Device You Want The Book On) Back Camera. The Back Camera Is The One You use as if you are taking a picture of someone.
2. Simply point your Camera at the QR code and 'tap' the QR code with your finger to focus the camera.
3. A link / pop up will appear. Simply tap that (and make sure you have internet connection) and the FREE PDF containing all of the coloured images should appear.
4. Now you have access to these FOREVER. Simply 'Bookmark' The tab it opened on, or download the document and take wherever you want.
5. Repeat this on any device you want it on! (If you want it on a laptop, simply email the document to yourself!)

Any issues please email us at:
vicandersonpublishing@gmail.com
and we will be happy to help!!

Side Recipes

HONEY BUTTER BISCUITS

These handmade biscuits have a soft texture and a lot of buttery, flaky components. Even better, you probably already have the ingredients for this family recipe in your kitchen as they are common pantry basics. This simple handmade biscuit recipe deserves a permanent place in your recipe collection. No shortening is used in this recipe, only butter!

 PREPARATION TIME: **10 MINUTES** | COOKING TIME: **15 MINUTES**

SERVING SIZE: **2** | PER SERVING: **KCAL: 586; FAT: 17G; CARBS: 90G; PROTEIN: 18G; SUGARS: 16G; FIBRE: 3G**

Ingredients:

For the biscuits:

- 200g self-raising flour, plus more for dusting
- ½ tsp. granulated sugar
- 1 tbsp. cold unsalted butter
- 200 ml buttermilk, shaken
- Melted butter for brushing

For the honey butter:

- 1 tbsp. unsalted butter, at room temperature
- 1 tsp. honey
- ½ tsp. rock salt or to taste

Instructions:

Step 1: Preheat the air fryer to 160°C.

For the biscuits:

Step 2: In a large bowl, mix the flour and sugar. Add the cold butter and use your hands to mix until it resembles breadcrumbs. Pour in the buttermilk and mix until smooth dough forms.

Step 3: Roll the dough out to 3-cm thickness. Using a round cookie cutter, cut out 10 to 12 rounds from the mixture. Brush their tops with butter.

Step 4: Place the biscuits in the air fryer basket and bake for 15 minutes or until they are golden and the biscuits are soft within.

For the honey butter:

Step 5: Meanwhile, in a small bowl, mix the butter, honey, and salt until smooth.

Step 6: Take out the biscuits when they are ready and let them cool.

Step 7: Serve the biscuits with the honey butter.

GARLIC BREAD

The BEST garlic bread recipe shouldn't be cumbersome. Hence, making it in the air fryer makes life all the easier. Simply coat the bread with the seasoning and bake. No foil wrapping, no extra fuss.

 PREPARATION TIME: **10 MINUTES** | COOKING TIME: **3 MINUTES**

 SERVING SIZE: **2** | PER SERVING: **KCAL: 467; FAT: 29G; CARBS: 42G; PROTEIN: 10G; SUGARS: 1G; FIBRE: 2G**

Ingredients:

- 60g softened butter
- 4 tbsp. grated Parmesan cheese
- 2 garlic cloves, minced
- 1 tsp. dried parsley flakes
- 8 slices French or ciabatta bread

Instructions:

Step 1: Preheat the air fryer to 160°C.

Step 2: In a bowl, mix the butter, Parmesan cheese, garlic, and parsley. Spread the butter on both sides of the bread slices.

Step 3: Place the bread slices in the air fryer basket and bake for 2 to 3 minutes or until golden and crusty.

Step 4: Remove the garlic bread from the air fryer and serve warm.

CAULIFLOWER CHEESE BITES

These low-carb and nutritious cauliflower bites are made with a few ingredients but are herby, buttery, and creamy. While they serve well as side dishes, you can enjoy them as appetisers or snacks. They pack an array of flavours that will make you love cauliflower better.

PREPARATION TIME: 10 MINUTES | **COOKING TIME: 13 MINUTES**

SERVING SIZE: 2 | **PER SERVING: KCAL: 265; FAT: 15G; CARBS: 21G; PROTEIN: 14G; SUGARS: 4G; FIBRE: 4G**

Ingredients:

For the cauliflower:

- 2 eggs
- 4 tbsp. panko breadcrumbs
- 3 tbsp. grated Parmesan cheese
- 2 tsp. smoky chipotle spice
- Salt and black pepper to taste
- 200g cauliflower, cut into florets
- Cooking spray

For cheese sauce:

- 2 tsp. butter
- 2 garlic cloves, minced
- 2 tbsp. soured cream
- 2 tbsp. grated Parmesan cheese
- Salt and black pepper to taste
- 1 green onion, sliced

Instructions:

Step 1: Preheat the air fryer to 160°C.

Step 2: Crack the eggs into a bowl and whisk well. On a plate, mix the breadcrumbs, Parmesan cheese, chipotle spice, salt, and black pepper.

Step 3: Dip the cauliflower in the eggs and then coat in the Parmesan mixture. After, mist them with cooking spray.

Step 4: Arrange the cauliflower in the air fryer basket and fry for 4 to 5 minutes per side or until they are golden and tender.

For the cheese sauce:

Step 5: In a small saucepan, melt the butter and sauté the garlic for 1 minute or until fragrant. Stir in the sour cream and cheese until the cheese melts. Season with salt and black pepper.

Step 6: Remove the cauliflower onto a platter and drizzle the sauce on top.

Step 7: Garnish with the green onion and serve right away.

STUFFED MUSHROOMS

If you aren't big on mushrooms, these stuffed mushrooms may make you like them more. They bake with much crisp and a stuffing that would impress you. These herb and cheese stuffed mushrooms are as tasty as they get. They pair well with fish and chicken, and on some days are great as appetisers or snacks.

⏱ PREPARATION TIME: **10 MINUTES** | 🍲 COOKING TIME: **10 MINUTES**

🍽 SERVING SIZE: **2** | PER SERVING: **KCAL: 306; FAT: 22G; CARBS: 16G; PROTEIN: 14G; SUGARS: 4G; FIBRE: 2G**

Ingredients:

- 4 tbsp. breadcrumbs
- 4 tbsp. grated Pecorino Romano
- 2 tbsp. grated mozzarella
- 1 tbsp. chopped fresh parsley
- 1 tsp. chopped fresh mint
- 1 garlic clove, minced
- 2 tbsp. olive oil
- Salt and black pepper to taste
- 16 white button mushrooms, stems removed

Instructions:

Step 1: Preheat the air fryer to 170°C.

Step 2: In a bowl, combine all the ingredients except for half of the olive oil and the mushrooms. Season the mushrooms with the remaining olive oil and season with salt and black pepper. Spoon the cheese mixture into the mushrooms.

Step 3: Place the mushrooms in the air fryer and bake for 10 minutes or until the mushrooms are golden and tender.

Step 4: Plate the mushrooms and serve them warm.

AIR FRYER ASPARAGUS

These garlicky asparagus are so addictive, you may end up having them quite often. They are so yummy, you could even enjoy them as a snack. This recipe is straightforward and gets you crisp and soft asparagus in very little time.

⏱ PREPARATION TIME: **10 MINUTES** | 🍲 COOKING TIME: **6 MINUTES**

🍽 SERVING SIZE: **2** | PER SERVING: **KCAL: 133; FAT: 11G; CARBS: 9G; PROTEIN: 4G; SUGARS: 3G; FIBRE: 3G**

Ingredients:

- 2 tbsp. mayonnaise
- 1 tbsp. olive oil
- 2 tsp. minced garlic
- 2 tsp. grated lemon zest
- ½ tsp. seasoned salt
- ½ tsp. black pepper or to taste
- 220g fresh asparagus, trimmed
- 1 tbsp. grated Parmesan cheese
- Lemon wedges for serving

Instructions:

Step 1: Preheat the air fryer to 180°C.

Step 2: In a bowl, mix the mayonnaise, olive oil, garlic, lemon zest, black pepper, and seasoned salt. Add the asparagus and coat with the mixture.

Step 3: Lay the asparagus in the air fryer basket and cook for 4 to 6 minutes or until lightly browned and tender.

Step 4: Plate the asparagus and sprinkle the Parmesan cheese on top.

Step 5: Serve them warm with lemon wedges.

VEGETARIAN PUMPKIN SCHNITZEL

During autumn, make sure to try this pumpkin treat. It is well-crisped on the outside with buttery pumpkin bites on the inside, with cheddar, nuts, and parsley for rich bites. Enjoy it with a salad or as a snack by itself.

⏱ PREPARATION TIME: **10 MINUTES** | 🍲 COOKING TIME: **10 MINUTES**

🍽 SERVING SIZE: **2** | PER SERVING: **KCAL: 402; FAT: 15G; CARBS: 51G; PROTEIN: 16G; SUGARS: 7G; FIBRE: 4G**

Ingredients:

- 120g panko breadcrumbs
- 2 tbsp. finely grated cheddar cheese
- 1 tbsp. filberts or hazelnuts, finely chopped
- 1 tbsp. flat-leaf parsley, plus additional to serve
- 200g pumpkin, peeled and cut into slices
- 1 egg, beaten
- Olive oil for coating
- Lemon wedges for serving

Instructions:

Step 1: Preheat the air fryer to 180°C.

Step 2: On a plate, mix the breadcrumbs, cheddar, filberts or hazelnuts, and parsley.

Step 3: Dip the pumpkin slices in egg and coat well in the breadcrumb mixture.

Step 4: Coat the air fryer basket with olive oil and place the pumpkin in it. Air fry for 8 to 10 minutes or until they are golden and buttery tender within.

Step 5: Take them out and serve warm with lemon wedges and potato mash.

COURGETTE CHIPS

Courgette chips are healthy. So, you can have them instead of French fries. They are also delicious, crunchy, and perfectly paleo. These simple baked courgette chips with cheese are just irresistible. They are ideal for children and adults alike, and can be enjoyed as a snack option too.

PREPARATION TIME: **10 MINUTES** | COOKING TIME: **10 MINUTES**

SERVING SIZE: **2** | PER SERVING: **KCAL: 243; FAT: 10G; CARBS: 25G; PROTEIN: 13G; SUGARS: 1G; FIBRE: 2G**

Ingredients:

- 4 tbsp. panko breadcrumbs
- 4 tbsp. Parmesan cheese, finely grated
- 1 tsp. dried herb mix
- ½ tsp. paprika
- Salt and black pepper to taste
- 4 tbsp. plain flour
- 2 eggs, lightly beaten
- 4 courgettes, cut into 3-cm-thick sticks
- Olive oil for coating

Instructions:

Step 1: Preheat the air fryer to 200°C.

Step 2: On a plate, put the breadcrumbs, Parmesan cheese, herb mix, paprika, salt, and black pepper.

Step 3: Dredge the courgette sticks with flour, dip them in the eggs, and then coat well with the breadcrumb mixture.

Step 4: Coat the air fryer basket with oil and arrange the courgette sticks in it. Air fry for 4 to 5 minutes or until golden per side.

Please scan the QR code below to access your bonus PDF with all 150 recipes with full coloured photos & beautiful designs alongside! This is the only way we can get the recipes with coloured photos to you & keep the book as reasonably priced as possible.

Also, once downloaded you can take the PDF with you digitally wherever you go- meaning you can cook these recipes wherever you may be! (As long as you have an air fryer!)

We hope you enjoy and do let us know your feedback!

STEP BY STEP GUIDE TO ACCESS

1. Open Your Phones (Or Any Device You Want The Book On) Back Camera. The Back Camera Is The One You use as if you are taking a picture of someone.
2. Simply point your Camera at the QR code and 'tap' the QR code with your finger to focus the camera.
3. A link / pop up will appear. Simply tap that (and make sure you have internet connection) and the FREE PDF containing all of the coloured images should appear.
4. Now you have access to these FOREVER. Simply 'Bookmark' The tab it opened on, or download the document and take wherever you want.
5. Repeat this on any device you want it on! (If you want it on a laptop, simply email the document to yourself!)

Any issues please email us at:
vicandersonpublishing@gmail.com
and we will be happy to help!!

Dessert
Recipes

CELEBRATION BITES

These chocolate-stuffed puff pastries have a lot to love. They're simple, efficient, and delectable! You can make dessert in no time by using a few sheets of pre-made puff pastry, some chocolate pieces, and a light sprinkle of icing sugar. You can make this ideal pastry on the go and enjoy it with a late cup of coffee.

⏱ PREPARATION TIME: **10 MINUTES** 🍲 COOKING TIME: **9 MINUTES**

🍽 SERVING SIZE: **2** | PER SERVING: **KCAL: 1,003; FAT: 69G; CARBS: 93G; PROTEIN: 12G; SUGARS: 59G; FIBRE: 8G**

Ingredients:

- 4 sheets frozen thin crust pastry, thawed
- 1 egg, lightly beaten
- 24 Mars Celebrations-size chocolates
- Cinnamon sugar for topping
- Icing sugar for dusting
- Whipped cream for serving

Instructions:

Step 1: Preheat the air fryer to 190°C.

Step 2: Cut each pastry into six rectangles. Brush the pastry rectangles with egg. Place one chocolate piece in the centre of each rectangle. Fold the pastry over the chocolate, trim the edges of the pastry, and seal the edges.

Step 3: Place the dough parcels on baking paper and sprinkle the cinnamon sugar on top.

Step 4: Line the air fryer basket with baking paper and arrange the dough parcels in it. Bake for 8 to 9 minutes or until the pastry is golden and crusty.

Step 5: Transfer the chocolate parcels to a wire rack and dust with icing sugar. Serve warm.

FRIED OREOS

Oreos have such great taste that frying them seems like a lot—but they are delicious and can be paired with creamy sweet sauces. The Oreo cookies are dipped in flour batter and then fried until they are golden and crispy.

⏱ PREPARATION TIME: **10 MINUTES** | 🍲 COOKING TIME: **7 MINUTES**

🍽 SERVING SIZE: **2** | PER SERVING: **KCAL: 605; FAT: 19G; CARBS: 94G; PROTEIN: 13G; SUGARS: 29G; FIBRE: 3G**

Ingredients:

- 1 large egg
- 4 tbsp. milk
- 1 tsp. pure vanilla extract
- 250g pancake and baking mix, plus additional amounts as necessary
- 2 tsp. sugar
- 12 Oreos
- Icing sugar

Instructions:

Step 1: Preheat the air fryer to 160°C.

Step 2: Crack the egg into a bowl and whisk with the milk, vanilla, pancake mix, and sugar until smooth and thick.

Step 3: Line the air fryer basket with baking paper.

Step 4: Dip the Oreos in the batter to coat fully and place them on the baking paper in the air fryer in a single layer. Bake for 7 minutes or until golden and the batter has set.

Step 5: Transfer them to a wire rack to cool and if you have any extras, bake them as well. Enjoy!

CHOCOLATE CHIP OATMEAL COOKIES

These yummy chocolate chip oatmeal cookies make fine additions to your dessert and snack collection. With top notes of chocolate and butter, these oatmeal cookies are addictive. They are crunchy on the outside and chewy on the inside, as every great cookie should be.

⏱ PREPARATION TIME: **10 MINUTES** | 🍲 COOKING TIME: **10 MINUTES**

🍽 SERVING SIZE: **2** | PER SERVING: **KCAL: 602; FAT: 23G; CARBS: 85G; PROTEIN: 14G; SUGARS: 33G; FIBRE: 8G**

Ingredients:

- 4 tbsp. softened butter
- 4 tbsp. sugar
- 70g brown sugar
- 1 large egg, cracked into a bowl
- 1 tsp. vanilla extract
- 220g quick oats
- 4 tbsp. plain flour
- 2 tbsp. custard powder
- ½ tsp. baking soda
- ¼ tsp. salt
- 4 tbsp. semisweet chocolate chips

Instructions:

Step 1: Preheat the air fryer to 170°C.

Step 2: In a bowl, cream the butter and both sugars until light and creamy. Add the egg and vanilla. Whisk until smooth.

Step 3: In another bowl, combine the oats, flour, custard powder, baking soda, and salt. Combine the wet and dry ingredients and whisk until smooth. Fold in the chocolate chips.

Step 4: Line the air fryer basket with baking paper. Add 1 tbsp. dollop of the dough on the baking paper with intervals between them.

Step 5: Bake for 8 to 10 minutes or until the cookies set.

Step 6: Transfer them to a wire rack to cool and bake any remaining batter.

Step 7: Enjoy!

....

MARBLE LATTICE

Marble lattice is a classic! A yummy dessert with melted marbled chocolate gushing from it and a beautiful lattice on top. A full block of marble chocolate is wrapped in a beautiful puff pastry lattice and air-fried to golden perfection. Serve it with ice cream.

⏱ PREPARATION TIME: **10 MINUTES** | 🍲 COOKING TIME: **10 MINUTES**

🍽 SERVING SIZE: **2** | PER SERVING: **KCAL: 504; FAT: 32G; CARBS: 45G; PROTEIN: 9G; SUGARS: 21G; FIBRE: 2G**

Ingredients:

- 80g marble chocolate block, cut in halves
- 1 egg, lightly beaten
- 2 sheets of thawed frozen puff pastry
- Ice cream for serving

Instructions:

Step 1: Preheat the air fryer to 180°C.

Step 2: Place one chocolate at the centre of each puff pastry sheet. Brush the edges of the pastry with egg and wrap it over the chocolate. Trim the edges (don't discard) and seal the edges.

Step 3: Cut the trimmed pastry pieces into strips. Make a lattice on the pastry with the pastry strips and brush the top with egg.

Step 4: Place the pastries in the air fryer and bake for 10 minutes or until golden.

Step 5: Transfer them to a wire rack to slightly cool and serve with ice cream.

PEPPERMINT LAVA CAKES

The ideal decadent, handcrafted winter dessert. These chocolate molten lava cakes are filled with peppermint white chocolate. A real treat to beat the chill. Such a decadent winter treat in miniature size.

⏱ PREPARATION TIME: **10 MINUTES** | 🍲 COOKING TIME: **12 MINUTES**

🍽 SERVING SIZE: **2** | PER SERVING: **KCAL: 976; FAT: 65G; CARBS: 93G; PROTEIN: 15G; SUGARS: 76G; FIBRE: 6G**

Ingredients:

- 200g semisweet chocolate chips
- 4 tbsp. cubed butter
  + extra for greasing
- 4 tbsp. icing sugar
- 2 large eggs, room temperature, cracked into a bowl
- 2 large egg yolks, room temperature
- 1 tsp. peppermint extract
- 2 tbsp. plain flour
- 1 tbsp. peppermint white chocolate, crushed
  + extra for garnish

Instructions:

Step 1: Preheat the air fryer to 180°C.

Step 2: In a safe microwave bowl, add the chocolate chips and butter. Melt them in the microwave for 30 seconds. Take the bowl out and stir until creamy. Let cool to touch.

Step 3: Add the icing sugar, eggs, egg yolks, and peppermint extract. Whisk until smooth. Add the flour and mix until smooth.

Step 4: Grease 4 small ramekins with butter. Pour the batter into the ramekins halfway, add the crushed peppermint white chocolate, and pour on the remaining batter.

Step 5: Place the ramekins in the air fryer and bake for 10 to 12 minutes or until the batter sets.

Step 6: Take out the ramekins and let cool.

Step 7: Garnish with crushed peppermint white chocolate and serve.

Please scan the QR code below to access your bonus PDF with all 150 recipes with full coloured photos & beautiful designs alongside! This is the only way we can get the recipes with coloured photos to you & keep the book as reasonably priced as possible.

Also, once downloaded you can take the PDF with you digitally wherever you go- meaning you can cook these recipes wherever you may be! (As long as you have an air fryer!)

We hope you enjoy and do let us know your feedback!

STEP BY STEP GUIDE TO ACCESS

1. Open Your Phones (Or Any Device You Want The Book On) Back Camera. The Back Camera Is The One You use as if you are taking a picture of someone.
2. Simply point your Camera at the QR code and 'tap' the QR code with your finger to focus the camera.
3. A link / pop up will appear. Simply tap that (and make sure you have internet connection) and the FREE PDF containing all of the coloured images should appear.
4. Now you have access to these FOREVER. Simply 'Bookmark' The tab it opened on, or download the document and take wherever you want.
5. Repeat this on any device you want it on! (If you want it on a laptop, simply email the document to yourself!)

Any issues please email us at:
vicandersonpublishing@gmail.com
and we will be happy to help!!

Vegan Recipes

ACORN SQUASH SLICES

If you haven't gotten around to eating acorn squash, you should try roasting them in the air fryer. This sweet buttery version will please your breakfast platter. Squash is one of those ingredients that doesn't require much preparation to taste nice. I think roasting is perfect for it as it allows its natural flavour to come through. Here, I boost the aroma with sweet butter.

⏱ PREPARATION TIME: **10 MINUTES** | 🍲 COOKING TIME: **13 MINUTES**

🍽 SERVING SIZE: **2** | PER SERVING: **KCAL: 444; FAT: 24G; CARBS: 63G; PROTEIN: 4G; SUGARS: 18G; FIBRE: 7G**

Ingredients:

- 2 little acorn squash, halved, deseeded, and sliced
- 4 tbsp. brown sugar
- 4 tbsp. softened vegan butter
- Olive oil for coating

Instructions:

Step 1: Preheat the air fryer to 160°C.

Step 2: Coat the air fryer basket with olive oil and arrange the squash in it in a single layer. Roast for 5 minutes per side.

Step 3: In a bowl, mix the brown sugar and vegan butter. Spread the sweet butter on the squash and bake for 3 more minutes or until golden.

Step 4: Plate the squash and serve warm.

BANANA MUFFINS

Banana muffins are a great way to use up overly ripened bananas. They are a breakfast favourite and you can tuck them in your snack pack for later munching too. These banana muffins are made with simple ingredients that you can grab from your pantry. They pack a ton of flavour and are freezable too. Meaning, you can batch make and microwave them whenever you want them.

⏱ PREPARATION TIME: **10 MINUTES** | 🍲 COOKING TIME: **10 MINUTES**

🍽 SERVING SIZE: **2** | PER SERVING: **KCAL: 495; FAT: 31G; CARBS: 51G; PROTEIN: 8G; SUGARS: 6G; FIBRE: 4G**

Ingredients:

- 2 ripe bananas, peeled
- 4 tbsp. self-raising flour
- 2 tbsp. maple sugar
- 60 ml vegan egg
- 4 tbsp. olive oil
- 4 tbsp. vegan buttermilk
- Maple syrup for brushing

Instructions:

Step 1: Preheat the air fryer to 180°C.

Step 2: Mash the bananas in a bowl using a fork until smooth. Set it aside.

Step 3: In a bowl, mix the flour and maple sugar. In another bowl, whisk the vegan egg, olive oil, vegan buttermilk, and mashed bananas until smooth. Combine both mixtures until smooth batter forms.

Step 4: Pour the batter into 4 lined muffin cups. Place the muffin cups in the air fryer and bake for 8 to 10 minutes or until set within when a toothpick is inserted into them.

Step 5: Take out the muffin cups and let rest for 4 minutes. Pop out the muffins and let cool to your desire on a wire rack.

Step 6: Brush their tops with maple syrup and serve.

BREAD

Everyone needs some kind of bread at home. Making bread at home may not be your first choice, but this super easy recipe will get you a loaf in little time. A perfect make for your toast, sandwiches, and croutons. Once you try this recipe, you won't want to bake bread any other way. It is completely delicious too.

 PREPARATION TIME: **1 HOUR 10 MINUTES** | COOKING TIME: **20 MINUTES**

SERVING SIZE: **2** | PER SERVING: **KCAL: 681; FAT: 13G; CARBS: 120G; PROTEIN: 18G; SUGARS: 5G; FIBRE: 5G**

Ingredients:

- 2 tbsp. melted vegan unsalted butter, plus additional for the pan
- 250 ml warm water (41-46°C)
- 1 tbsp. dried active yeast
- 2 tsp. sugar
- ½ tsp. salt
- 300g plain flour

Instructions:

Step 1: Preheat the air fryer to 190°C.

Step 2: In the bowl of a stand mixer with the dough hook attached, mix the vegan butter, warm water, yeast, sugar, and salt on low speed. Add 150g of flour at a time. Once incorporated, increase the speed to medium and whisk until smooth, sticky dough forms. Cover the bowl and let it rise for 1 hour.

Step 3: Brush a loaf pan with vegan butter and place the dough in it.

Step 4: Place the loaf pan in the air fryer basket and bake for 20 minutes or until golden, crusty, and fluffy within.

Step 5: Take out the loaf pan and let the bread rest in the pan for 5 minutes. Transfer the bread to a wire rack and let it rest completely.

Step 6: Slice the bread and serve.

· ·

VEGGIE AND HOUMOUS SANDWICH

Sometimes, you need a loaded sandwich in the morning when the hunger pangs are fired up. This houmous sandwich packed with vegetables will satisfy you well. Houmous isn't meant for snack time or appetisers only. You can slather an inviting portion on toasted bread and build a delightful vegetable sandwich.

 PREPARATION TIME: **10 MINUTES** | COOKING TIME: **4 MINUTES**

 SERVING SIZE: **2** | PER SERVING: **KCAL: 196; FAT: 7G; CARBS: 28G; PROTEIN: 7G; SUGARS: 5G; FIBRE: 7G**

Ingredients:

- 2 slices whole-grain vegan bread
- 2 tbsp. houmous
- A handful of mixed salad greens
- ¼ avocado, peeled, pitted, and sliced
- 1 medium tomato, sliced
- 2 cucumber slices
- 2 tbsp. grated carrot

Instructions:

Step 1: Preheat the air fryer to 160°C.

Step 2: Coat the air fryer basket with cooking oil and place the bread slices in it. Toast for 1 to 2 minutes or until nicely browned.

Step 3: Plate the toast and spread the houmous on one side of each slice. Top one slice with the salad greens avocado, tomato, cucumber, and carrot. Cover with the other slice with the houmous side facing inwards.

Step 4: Slice the sandwich in half diagonally and serve.

MAPLE WALNUT CINNAMON ROLL UPS

This cinnamon-flavoured dessert has a similar flavour to baklava, but requires far less effort to make; thanks to its simple components. Cinnamon is such a unique spice and you either like it or don't. But in these maple walnut cinnamon roll ups, cinnamon merges well with maple sugar for a fantastic flavour. So, I believe you'll love it. This recipe serves 8 or more.

 PREPARATION TIME: **10 MINUTES** | COOKING TIME: **12 MINUTES**

 SERVING SIZE: **2** | PER SERVING: **KCAL: 562; FAT: 45G; CARBS: 37G; PROTEIN: 7G; SUGARS: 17G; FIBRE: 3G**

Ingredients:

For the roll ups:

- 250g toasted ground walnuts
- 4 tbsp. maple sugar
- 1 tbsp. cinnamon powder
- 12 sheets of thawed frozen filo pastry (vegan)
- 250 ml melted vegan butter

For the syrup:

- 4 tbsp. maple syrup
- 4 tbsp. granulated sugar
- 120 ml water
- 1 tsp. fresh lemon juice

Instructions:

Step 1: Preheat the air fryer to 165°C.

Step 2: In a bowl, mix the walnuts, maple sugar, and cinnamon.

Step 3: Lay one sheet of filo pastry on baking paper. Brush with vegan butter and lay another sheet of filo pastry on top. Now, spread some of the walnut mixture on top and starting from the longer side, roll the dough over the filling. Slice into 4 smaller rolls. Repeat making more rolls the same way with the remaining filo pastry sheets and walnut mixture. Use toothpicks to secure the edges and brush all the rolls with butter.

Step 4: Line the air fryer basket with baking paper and place some rolls on the baking paper in a single layer. Bake for 9 to 12 minutes or until golden and risen.

Step 5: Transfer the rolls to a wire rack and remove the toothpicks. Bake the remaining rolls.

For the syrup:

Step 6: In a bowl, mix the maple syrup, sugar, water, and lemon juice until smooth.

Step 7: Drizzle the syrup over the rolls, top with any remaining walnut mixture, and serve.

QUINOA ARANCINI

You can't go wrong in taste with these cute quinoa arancini as light breakfast bites. Make a ton and extend their use to snack time. They are super healthy and filling. These scrumptious vegan arancini will appeal to even the most ardent meat eater. They run out fast, so always make enough.

⏱ PREPARATION TIME: **10 MINUTES** | 🍲 COOKING TIME: **8 MINUTES**

🍽 SERVING SIZE: **2** | PER SERVING: **KCAL: 700; FAT: 24G; CARBS: 89G; PROTEIN: 31G; SUGARS: 6G; FIBRE: 9G**

Ingredients:

- 400g cooked quinoa
- 60 ml vegan egg
- 120g seasoned breadcrumbs
- 4 tbsp. finely grated vegan Parmesan cheese
- 1 tbsp. olive oil
- 1 tbsp. minced fresh basil leaves
- ½ tsp. garlic powder
- ½ tsp. black pepper
- ½ tsp. salt
- 60g grated vegan mozzarella cheese

Instructions:

Step 1: Preheat the air fryer to 180°C.

Step 2: Add all the ingredients to a bowl and mix well. Form 6 balls from the mixture. Dip the quinoa balls in the vegan egg and coat it in the breadcrumbs. Coat the quinoa balls with cooking spray.

Step 3: Place the quinoa balls in the air fryer basket and fry for 3 to 4 minutes per side or until golden.

Step 4: Transfer the quinoa balls to a bowl and serve warm.

BAKED POTATOES

These loaded baked potatoes are a must make with the air fryer because they fill you up quite well. The skin of the potatoes bakes with a crunch and the flesh is buttery soft that melts in your mouth. They are really worth the wait. Once they are ready and topped with a helping of cashew cream and other favourite toppings, you know they'll be finished in no time.

⏱ PREPARATION TIME: **10 MINUTES** | 🍲 COOKING TIME: **15 MINUTES**

🍽 SERVING SIZE: **2** | PER SERVING: **KCAL: 97; FAT: 0G; CARBS: 22G; PROTEIN: 3G; SUGARS: 1G; FIBRE: 3G**

Ingredients:

- 250g baby potatoes, scrubbed and halved lengthwise
- 1 tsp. chopped fresh rosemary
- Salt to taste
- Cashew cream and sweet chilli sauce for serving

Instructions:

Step 1: Preheat the air fryer to 180°C.

Step 2: Season the potatoes with rosemary and salt.

Step 3: Coat the air fryer basket with cooking oil and place the potatoes, with the open side facing upwards. Bake for 15 minutes or until the skin is crispy and the skin is cooked, flipping halfway.

Step 4: Take out the potatoes and top with cashew cream and sweet chilli sauce.

VEGAN FRENCH TOAST

This is the BEST vegan French toast recipe. Simple to prepare in only 10 minutes with common ingredients, you won't even notice the absence of eggs in this delectable weekend meal. This French toast is wonderfully crisp, thick, and perfect thanks to the sweet blueberry drizzle that sits atop it.

 PREPARATION TIME: **10 MINUTES** | COOKING TIME: **16 MINUTES**

SERVING SIZE: **2** | PER SERVING: **KCAL: 288; FAT: 11G; CARBS: 36G; PROTEIN: 12G; SUGARS: 16G; FIBRE: 2G**

Ingredients:

- 1 tbsp. maple sugar
- 2 tbsp. blueberries
- 60 ml vegan egg
- 1 tbsp. gram flour
- ½ tsp. cinnamon powder
- 100 ml oat milk or rice milk
- 1 tbsp. golden caster sugar
- ½ tsp. vanilla extract
- 4 thick slices of white bread
- Olive oil, for air frying
- Icing sugar, for dusting

Instructions:

Step 1: Preheat the air fryer to 160°C.

Step 2: Add maple sugar and blueberries to a pot and cook over medium heat for 5 to 8 minutes or until the blueberries break. Turn the heat off and let cool. Strain the syrup into a bowl and discard the solids.

Step 3: In a bowl, whisk the remaining ingredients except for the bread slices and olive oil. Dip the bread in the toast for 3 minutes, flip the bread, and let soak for 3 more minutes.

Step 4: Coat the air fryer basket with olive oil and lay the bread pieces in the basket. Bake for 3 to 4 minutes per side or until golden and the toast is no longer soggy.

Step 5: Transfer the bread to a plate and drizzle the blueberry syrup on top. Dust the toasts with icing sugar and serve warm.

GARLIC ROSEMARY BRUSSELS SPROUTS

These super healthy veggies are made uniquely here. Besides being flavoured with rosemary and garlic, they are drizzled with breadcrumbs for added crunch. They turn out golden and flavour-packed with a fine garlic herb boost.

 PREPARATION TIME: **8 MINUTES** | COOKING TIME: **12 MINUTES**

 SERVING SIZE: **2** | PER SERVING: **KCAL: 469; FAT: 18G; CARBS: 67G; PROTEIN: 16G; SUGARS: 9G; FIBRE: 12G**

Ingredients:

- 450g Brussels sprouts, trimmed and halved
- 2 tbsp. olive oil
- 2 garlic cloves, minced
- Salt and black pepper to taste
- 1 tbsp. minced fresh rosemary
- 125g panko breadcrumbs

Instructions:

Step 1: Preheat the air fryer to 160°C.

Step 2: In a bowl, combine the Brussels sprouts, olive oil, garlic, salt, black pepper, rosemary, and breadcrumbs. Toss well.

Step 3: Add the Brussels sprouts to the air fryer basket and roast for 10 to 12 minutes while shaking the basket halfway until golden and tender.

Step 4: Plate them and serve warm.

CUMIN-FLAVOURED CARROTS

These soft, flavourful, and buttery roasted carrots, which are seasoned with thyme, rosemary, garlic, and cumin, are sure to be the highlight of Sunday dinner. With ingredients you likely already have on hand, this carrot side dish comes together quickly.

⏱ PREPARATION TIME: **10 MINUTES** | 🍲 COOKING TIME: **15 MINUTES**

🍽 SERVING SIZE: **2** | PER SERVING: **KCAL: 147; FAT: 7G; CARBS: 21G; PROTEIN: 2G; SUGARS: 10G; FIBRE: 6G**

Ingredients:

- 400g carrots, peeled and sliced into 4 ½-inch sticks
- 1 tbsp. coconut oil
- 1 tsp. ground coriander
- 1 tsp. ground cumin
- 2 garlic cloves, minced
- Salt and black pepper to taste
- Minced fresh coriander for garnish

Instructions:

Step 1: Preheat the air fryer to 160°C.

Step 2: Add the carrots to a large bowl and toss with the coconut oil, coriander, cumin, garlic, salt, and black pepper.

Step 3: Place them in the air fryer in a single layer and bake for 12 to 15 minutes or until they are slightly brown and crisp-tender; turn them halfway through cooking.

Step 4: Plate the carrots and garnish with coriander. Serve warm.

....

CRISPY POTATO CHIPS

After having these potato chips, you won't be lured by the store-bought ones anymore. They turn out as crispy as expected and what's better, you control the seasoning that you use for them. For lunch, enjoy them with soup. It only takes 10 minutes to make these crunchy, crispy potato chips. Season them as you like. I use some lemon zest and paprika here.

⏱ PREPARATION TIME: **15 MINUTES** | 🍲 COOKING TIME: **30 MINUTES**

🍽 SERVING SIZE: **2** | PER SERVING: **KCAL: 225; FAT: 7G; CARBS: 38G; PROTEIN: 4G; SUGARS: 2G; FIBRE: 5G**

Ingredients:

- 2 Yukon gold potatoes, peeled
- 1 tbsp. olive oil
- Salt and black pepper to taste
- ¼ tsp. paprika
- ½ tbsp. fresh lemon zest

Instructions:

Step 1: Preheat the air fryer to 160°C.

Step 2: Using a mandoline, slice the potatoes very thinly and pat them dry with a paper towel. Add them to a bowl, drizzle on the olive oil, and season with salt and black pepper, paprika, and lemon zest. Toss well.

Step 3: Add a batch to the air fryer basket in a single or double layer. Fry for 20 to 30 minutes or until they are golden and crispy. Toss them every 5 minutes to ensure even cooking. Transfer any cooked piece to a large bowl.

Step 4: Add all the potatoes to the bowl when ready and season with salt. Enjoy!

GARLIC PATTY PAN SQUASH

Patty pan squash is a summer squash with scalloped edges that resembles miniature flying saucers. Despite their peculiar form, they are simple to slice and easy to prepare. Smaller is always better to use. Roasting is my preferred method for cooking vegetables, and patty pan squash is no exception. The taste of these adorable small vegetable discs is herby and moderate, making them great for pairing with other foods like soups.

 PREPARATION TIME: **10 MINUTES** | COOKING TIME: **15 MINUTES**

SERVING SIZE: **2** | PER SERVING: **KCAL: 106; FAT: 7G; CARBS: 10G; PROTEIN: 3G; SUGARS: 6G; FIBRE: 3G**

Ingredients:

- 500g small patty pan squash
- 1 tbsp. olive oil
- 2 garlic cloves, minced
- Salt and black pepper to taste
- ½ tsp. dried oregano
- ½ tsp. dried thyme
- 1 tbsp. minced fresh parsley for garnish

Instructions:

Step 1: Preheat the air fryer to 160°C.
Step 2: Add the patty pan squash to a large bowl and toss with the olive oil, garlic, salt, black pepper, oregano, and thyme.
Step 3: Put them in the air fryer in a single layer and bake for 12 to 15 minutes or until they are slightly brown and tender; turn them halfway through cooking.
Step 4: Plate the squash and garnish with parsley. Serve warm.

....

GARLIC MUSHROOMS

Mushrooms take on just about any seasoning that you want them to. I particularly love some garlic butter with them but on some days, olive oil, salt, and pepper are just perfect. These mushrooms are simply roasted and tossed in tarragon garlic butter for a simple but sophisticated serving.

 PREPARATION TIME: **10 MINUTES** | COOKING TIME: **12 MINUTES**

SERVING SIZE: **2** | PER SERVING: **KCAL: 65; FAT: 6G; CARBS: 3G; PROTEIN: 2G; SUGARS: 1G; FIBRE: 1G**

Ingredients:

- 12 white button mushrooms, stems removed
- 2 tsp. chopped fresh tarragon
- 1 tbsp. vegan butter, melted
- 2 garlic cloves, minced
- Salt and black pepper to taste

Instructions:

Step 1: Preheat the air fryer to 180°C.
Step 2: In a bowl, toss the mushrooms, tarragon, vegan butter, garlic, salt, and black pepper.
Step 3: Add the mushrooms to the air fryer basket and roast for 10 to 12 minutes while turning halfway until the mushrooms are tender.
Step 4: Plate them and serve warm.

RATATOUILLE AND PERSIAN VEGAN FETA FILO PARCELS

These little veggie-filled filo pastry packages are individuals, which means better structure for serving. They are packed with goodness—vegan feta, four veggies, and tasty pesto for serving. What's not to love? The buttery pastry bakes with such a golden and flaky feel. This recipe makes 12 parcels.

⏱ PREPARATION TIME: **15 MINUTES** | 🍲 COOKING TIME: **37 MINUTES**

🍽 SERVING SIZE: **2** | PER SERVING: **KCAL: 376; FAT: 30G; CARBS: 17G; PROTEIN: 11G; SUGARS: 4G; FIBRE: 2G**

Ingredients:

- 2 green onions, finely sliced
- 2 large courgettes, cut into 1 cm long slices.
- 1 red bell pepper, deseeded and cut into 1 cm-long chunks.
- 1 large aubergine, diced into 1 cm pieces
- 1 garlic clove, minced
- 2 tsp. olive oil
- 1 tbsp. red wine vinegar or sherry vinegar
- Salt and black pepper to taste
- 2 tbsp. chopped fresh parsley
- 2 tsp. plain flour
- 12 filo pastry sheets
- 4 tbsp. vegan butter, melted
- 4 tbsp. crumbled vegan feta
- Basil pesto for serving

Instructions:

Step 1: Preheat the air fryer to 200°C.

Step 2: In a bowl, combine the green onions, courgettes, bell pepper, aubergine, garlic, olive oil, vinegar, salt, and black pepper. Toss well.

Step 3: Add the vegetables to the air fryer basket and roast for 10 to 12 minutes or until lightly browned and tender. Transfer them to a plate when they are ready and mix in the parsley.

Step 4: Dust a clean, flat surface with flour and roll out the pastry sheets individually. Brush them with butter.

Step 5: Spoon the vegetables onto the centres of the pastry and top with the vegan feta. Wrap the pastry over the filling and seal the edges. Brush their tops with butter.

Step 6: Place the pastries in the air fryer basket and bake for 15 minutes or until they are golden and crusty.

Step 7: Take out the pastries, let them cool for a while, and serve them warm with basil pesto.

ROASTED GREEN BEANS

Given that they can be prepared in the air fryer in just 15 minutes, green beans are one of the quickest vegetable options to roast. And they are versatile for serving. Like all roasted vegetables, green beans have an enhanced, caramelised flavour that tastes more sophisticated than the raw or steamed forms. Hence, a simple seasoning goes a long way.

⏱ PREPARATION TIME: **10 MINUTES** | 🍲 COOKING TIME: **12 MINUTES**

🍽 SERVING SIZE: **2** | PER SERVING: **KCAL: 156; FAT: 8G; CARBS: 20G; PROTEIN: 7G; SUGARS: 9G; FIBRE: 6G**

Ingredients:

- 300g fresh green beans, trimmed and cut into 5 cm pieces
- 200g mushrooms, sliced
- 1 red onion, halved and thinly sliced
- 1 tbsp. olive oil
- 1 tsp. seasoning mix, your preferred choice
- Salt and black pepper to taste

Instructions:

Step 1: Preheat the air fryer to 180°C.
Step 2: In a bowl, toss the green beans, mushrooms, red onion, olive oil, seasoning mix, salt, and black pepper.
Step 3: Add the vegetables to the air fryer basket and roast for 10 to 12 minutes while stirring halfway until the vegetables are tender.
Step 4: Plate them and serve warm.

BAGEL AVOCADO FRIES

These avocado fries substitute crispy chicken strips. You can pair them with soup, rice, or salad. They provide a nice crunch for the evening.

⏱ PREPARATION TIME: **10 MINUTES** | 🍲 COOKING TIME: **8 MINUTES**

🍽 SERVING SIZE: **2** | PER SERVING: **KCAL: 373; FAT: 22G; CARBS: 33G; PROTEIN: 13G; SUGARS: 2G; FIBRE: 9G**

Ingredients:

- 4 tbsp. plain flour
- 2 large eggs
- 4 tbsp. panko breadcrumbs
- 1 tbsp. bagel seasoning
- 2 tsp. black and/or white sesame seeds
- 1 large, just ripe avocado, halved, pitted, peeled, and cut into 1-cm-thick slices
- Lime wedges, for serving

Instructions:

Step 1: Preheat the air fryer to 175°C.
Step 2: Spread the flour on a plate. Crack the eggs into a bowl and beat. On another plate, mix the breadcrumbs, seasoning, and sesame seeds.
Step 3: Dredge the avocado in flour, dip them in eggs, and then coat well in the breadcrumb mixture.
Step 4: Coat the air fryer basket with cooking spray. Place the avocados in the air fryer basket and fry for 6 to 8 minutes or until golden and crispy; turning halfway through cooking.
Step 5: Transfer the avocados to a plate and serve warm.

SPICY CARROTS

For your next lunch, use these spicy roasted carrots as a side dish. They are just as simple to make and have a far nicer flavour than steamed or boiled carrots. The carrots are seasoned, then baked in the air fryer until they are tender and flavourful. It is simple to customise spicy roasted carrots to your tastes. They might be extremely hot, extremely mild, or somewhere in between.

 PREPARATION TIME: **10 MINUTES** | COOKING TIME: **12 MINUTES**

SERVING SIZE: **2** | PER SERVING: **KCAL: 149; FAT: 8G; CARBS: 21G; PROTEIN: 3G; SUGARS: 8G; FIBRE: 9G**

Ingredients:

- 200g medium carrots, sliced into 5 cm slices; larger ones, chopped lengthwise
- 1 tbsp. melted vegan butter
- 1 tsp. light brown sugar
- ½ tsp. rock salt
- 4 tbsp. chilli powder
- ½ tsp. black pepper
- ¼ tsp. cayenne pepper or to taste
- 2 tsp. chopped fresh mint

Instructions:

Step 1: Preheat the air fryer to 160°C.
Step 2: Add all the ingredients to a bowl except for the mint. Toss well.
Step 3: Add the carrots to the air fryer basket and roast for 10 to 12 minutes while stirring halfway until the carrots are tender.
Step 4: Plate them and serve warm.

SPAGHETTI SQUASH

There is no food more wonderful if you are following a low-carb diet than spaghetti squash. It is quite simple to prepare, and there are countless ways to cook with it. It has a lot of vitamins and minerals, including manganese, vitamin C, and vitamin B6, and is low in calories and high in fibre.

 PREPARATION TIME: **8 MINUTES** | COOKING TIME: **30 MINUTES**

 SERVING SIZE: **2** | PER SERVING: **KCAL: 76; FAT: 7G; CARBS: 4G; PROTEIN: 1G; SUGARS: 2G; FIBRE: 1G**

Ingredients:

- 1 tbsp. olive oil
- 1 medium spaghetti squash, halved lengthwise and deseeded
- Salt and black pepper to taste

Instructions:

Step 1: Preheat the air fryer to 180°C.
Step 2: Drizzle the olive oil on the inner parts of the spaghetti squash and season with salt and black pepper.
Step 3: Place the squash halves in the air fryer and bake for 25 to 30 minutes or until tender.
Step 4: Remove the squash and use a fork to shred the flesh to resemble spaghetti strands.
Step 5: Serve warm with your favourite toppings or sauce.

BUTTERNUT SQUASH SOUP

Making butternut squash soup on late Sunday afternoons is one of my favourite autumnal customs.
Nothing is more soothing than fresh roasted veggie soup on a chilly evening.
This creamy, nutritious butternut squash soup dish is the best comfort food. Pair with some crusty bread.

⏱ PREPARATION TIME: **10 MINUTES** | 🍲 COOKING TIME: **15 MINUTES**

🍽 SERVING SIZE: **2** | PER SERVING: **KCAL: 414; FAT: 27G; CARBS: 44G; PROTEIN: 6G; SUGARS: 6G; FIBRE: 6G**

Ingredients:

- 500g butternut squash, peeled and chopped into 2-cm chunks
- 2 medium carrots, cut into 4-cm slices
- 1 orange bell pepper, deseeded, cut into 2-cm thick slices
- 1 medium onion, cut into four wedges
- 2 tbsp. olive oil
- ½ tsp. minced garlic
- ½ tsp. fresh ginger
- ½ tsp. dried thyme
- Salt and black pepper to taste
- 750 ml vegetable broth, low sodium
- 120 ml cashew cream, plus extra for topping
- Pumpkin seeds, roasted and salted, for serving
- Chopped chives for serving

Instructions:

Step 1: Preheat the air fryer to 180°C.

Step 2: In a large bowl, combine all the ingredients except for the vegetable broth, cashew cream, pumpkin seeds, and chives.

Step 3: Put the vegetables in the air fryer basket and roast for 12 to 15 minutes or until golden and tender.

Step 4: Transfer the vegetables to a blender and add the vegetable broth and cashew cream. Blend until smooth. Adjust the taste with salt and black pepper if needed.

Step 5: Pour the soup into serving bowls and top with cashew cream, pumpkin seeds, and chives. Serve warm.

CHILLI GARLIC TOFU

This tofu is crispy and easy to prepare, completely vegan, and packs some heat for character. It has strong flavours from the distinctive chilli seasoning. Enjoy it with some plain rice, fried rice, or even roasted vegetables.

⏱ PREPARATION TIME: **40 MINUTES** | 🍲 COOKING TIME: **16 MINUTES**

🍽 SERVING SIZE: **2** | PER SERVING: **KCAL: 286; FAT: 17G; CARBS: 14G; PROTEIN: 22G; SUGARS: 3G; FIBRE: 4G**

Ingredients:

- 240g firm tofu, pressed and cut into 2-cm slabs
- 1 tbsp. olive oil
- 4 tbsp. soy sauce, low-sodium
- Salt and black pepper
- 2 tsp. rice wine vinegar
- 2 tbsp. mirin
- 1 tsp. brown sugar
- 1 tbsp. chilli-garlic paste or to taste
- 1 tsp. corn flour
- 3 garlic cloves, crushed
- 2 scallions, finely sliced for garnish

Instructions:

Step 1: Combine all the ingredients in a bowl except for the scallions and let the tofu marinate for 30 minutes.

Step 2: Preheat the air fryer to 200°C.

Step 3: Place the tofu in the air fryer basket and cook for 6 to 8 minutes per side or until golden.

Step 4: Transfer the tofu to a plate and garnish with scallions.

Step 5: Serve warm.

GLUTEN-FREE CROUTONS

Making your gluten-free croutons at home is a terrific way to use up stale bread. Season them with some herbs, butter, salt, and black pepper and you have a hit for pairing with soups and salads.

⏱ PREPARATION TIME: **10 MINUTES** | 🍲 COOKING TIME: **7 MINUTES**

🍽 SERVING SIZE: **2** | PER SERVING: **KCAL: 402; FAT: 30G; CARBS: 27G; PROTEIN: 8G; SUGARS: 4G; FIBRE: 5G**

Ingredients:

- 120g whole grain bread, cubed into 1 ½ cm pieces
- 4 tbsp. olive oil
- ½ tsp. dried oregano
- ½ tsp. garlic granules
- Salt and black pepper to taste

Instructions:

Step 1: Preheat the air fryer to 160°C.

Step 2: Add all the ingredients to a bowl and toss well.

Step 3: Spread the bread in the air fryer basket and toast for 5 to 7 minutes or until golden and crispy.

Step 4: Spread the croutons on a tray to cool. Serve.

CHIMICHANGAS VEGAN

These chimichangas are made particularly to pair with paprika rice. They are rich with beans, vegetables, salsa, cheese, and herbs. A full plate will be so satisfying. If you were once a meat eater, then you'll love these loaded chimichangas that replicate meatloaf but rather pack much protein in a crispy shell.

⏱ PREPARATION TIME: **10 MINUTES** | 🍲 COOKING TIME: **10 MINUTES**

🍽 SERVING SIZE: **2** | PER SERVING: **KCAL: 415; FAT: 19G; CARBS: 54G; PROTEIN: 12G; SUGARS: 13G; FIBRE: 8G**

Ingredients:

- 1 tbsp. vegetable oil
- 1 red onion, thinly sliced
- 1 red bell pepper, deseeded and thinly sliced
- 1 green bell pepper, deseeded and thinly sliced
- 100g can of black beans, drained
- 120g can of sweetcorn, drained
- 4 tbsp. salsa
- 2 tsp. taco seasoning
- 2 tsp. coriander leaves
- 4 tbsp. grated vegan Mexican cheese mix
- 2 medium tortillas
- 1 tbsp. chipotle salsa
- 4 tbsp. vegan soured cream
- A handful of cherry tomatoes, chopped
- 1 small red onion, halved and thinly sliced
- Guacamole for serving (optional)

Instructions:

Step 1: Preheat the air fryer to 180°C.

Step 2: Heat the olive oil in a skillet over medium heat and sauté the onion and bell peppers for 3 minutes or until tender. Turn the heat off and stir in the beans, sweetcorn, salsa, taco seasoning, half of the coriander, and vegan cheese blend.

Step 3: Lay out the tortillas individually and spoon the vegetable mix at the centre of the tortillas. Fold the shorter ends of the tortillas of the filling and then from one side of each longer side, fold the tortillas over the filling. Mist the tortillas with cooking spray.

Step 4: Place the tortillas in the air fryer basket and fry for 10 minutes or until golden and crispy without turning halfway.

Step 5: Plate the chimichangas and top with vegan soured cream, cherry tomatoes, onion, and the remaining coriander.

Step 6: Serve warm with guacamole and rice.

MOROCCAN-SPICED CARROTS

We made some spicy carrots a few recipes earlier but here, you get a banger. These carrots hail from North Africa and if you like intense flavouring, you'd be impressed by these. Serve these yummy Moroccan-spiced carrots with grilled tofu.

PREPARATION TIME: **5 MINUTES** | COOKING TIME: **12 MINUTES**

SERVING SIZE: **2** | PER SERVING: **KCAL: 211; FAT: 12G; CARBS: 27G; PROTEIN: 4G; SUGARS: 16G; FIBRE: 7G**

Ingredients:

- For the carrots:
- 200g medium carrots, peeled, trimmed, and cut into 1 cm thick pieces on the bias
- 1 tbsp. olive oil
- ½ tsp. ground cinnamon
- ½ tsp. ground coriander
- ½ tsp. ground cumin
- ½ tsp. rock salt
- ½ tsp. smoked paprika
- 1 tbsp. fresh orange juice
- 1 tbsp. fresh lemon juice

For garnish:

- 4 tbsp. pomegranate seeds
- 1 tbsp. chopped toasted almonds
- Torn fresh mint leaves for garnish

Instructions:

Step 1: Preheat the air fryer to 160°C.

Step 2: Add all the carrot ingredients to a bowl and toss well.

Step 3: Add the carrots to the air fryer basket and roast for 10 to 12 minutes while stirring halfway until the carrots are tender.

Step 4: Plate them and garnish with pomegranate seeds, almonds, and mint. Serve warm.

PRIMAVERA ROASTED VEGETABLES

Primavera roasted vegetables are the ideal healthy midweek dinner option since they are colourful, nutritious, and vibrant. This delightful veggie mix goes well with eggless pasta and grated vegan Parmesan.

⏱ PREPARATION TIME: **10 MINUTES** | 🍲 COOKING TIME: **12 MINUTES**

🍽 SERVING SIZE: **2** | PER SERVING: **KCAL: 704; FAT: 47G; CARBS: 27G; PROTEIN: 45G; SUGARS: 3G; FIBRE: 3G**

Ingredients:

- 1 small summer squash, trimmed and sliced into ½ cm thick rounds
- 1 small courgette, trimmed and sliced into ½ cm thick rounds
- 1 small red bell pepper, deseeded, cut into 2-cm pieces
- 2 tsp. olive oil
- ½ tsp. finely chopped fresh rosemary
- Salt and black pepper to taste
- 3 tbsp. grated vegan Parmesan, plus more for serving
- Chopped fresh parsley for garnish

Instructions:

Step 1: Preheat the air fryer to 160°C.

Step 2: Add all the ingredients to a bowl except for the vegan Parmesan and parsley and toss well.

Step 3: Add the vegetables to the air fryer basket and roast for 10 to 12 minutes while stirring halfway until the vegetables are tender.

Step 4: Remove the vegetables into a bowl, top with the vegan Parmesan cheese, and parsley.

Step 5: Serve warm.

· ·

FRIED OREGANO RADISHES

I needed a different method to use my surplus radishes in the garden than just as a salad topper. These fried radishes turned out tasty. In less than 15 minutes, these low-carb radishes are ready as a replacement for potatoes.

⏱ PREPARATION TIME: **5 MINUTES** | 🍲 COOKING TIME: **12 MINUTES**

🍽 SERVING SIZE: **2** | PER SERVING: **KCAL: 193; FAT: 14G; CARBS: 17G; PROTEIN: 3G; SUGARS: 10G; FIBRE: 7G**

Ingredients:

- 800g radishes, quartered, trimmed, and cut into wedges
- 2 tbsp. olive oil
- 1 tsp. dried oregano
- Salt and black pepper to taste

Instructions:

Step 1: Preheat the air fryer to 160°C.

Step 2: Add all the ingredients to a bowl and toss well.

Step 3: Add the radishes to the air fryer basket and roast for 10 to 12 minutes while shaking the basket halfway until the radishes are golden and tender.

Step 4: Plate them and serve warm.

SEASONED TOFU

This isn't your ordinary tofu. The tofu is seasoned richly with soy or tamari sauce and spicy with some peppercorns for added flavour. It is perfect with rice and vegetables. It is a popular one at Chinese restaurants and here you get to make it well-crisped all by yourself.

PREPARATION TIME: **40 MINUTES** | COOKING TIME: **10 MINUTES**

SERVING SIZE: **2** | PER SERVING: **KCAL: 240; FAT: 9G; CARBS: 33G; PROTEIN: 10G; SUGARS: 14G; FIBRE: 3G**

Ingredients:

- 1 tsp. vegetable oil
- 1 spring onion, finely sliced
- 1 long red chilli, finely sliced (optional)
- 1 garlic clove, smashed
- 2 tbsp. gluten-free tamari or soy sauce, low-sodium
- 2 tbsp. caster sugar
- 1 tsp. sesame oil
- 1 tsp. flaked sea salt
- 2 tsp. black peppercorns, crushed
- 1 tsp. dried chilli flakes
- 90g of firm tofu, cut into 2-cm-long chunks.
- 3 tbsp. rice flour

Instructions:

Step 1: Preheat the air fryer to 160°C.

Step 2: In a bowl, combine all the ingredients except for the rice flour and tofu. Mix well and dip the tofu in the marinade. Let it marinate for 30 minutes.

Step 3: Remove the tofu from the marinade and coat in the rice flour.

Step 4: Coat the air fryer basket with cooking oil and lay in the tofu in a single layer. Bake for 3 to 5 minutes per side or until golden and crispy.

Step 5: Plate the tofu and serve warm.

STUFFED SWEET POTATOES

Baked stuffed sweet potatoes are a great way to get every food group in one dish. They act as a tasty vehicle. These super spuds, which are high in fibre, vitamins, and minerals, are incredibly delicious too. Consider sweet potatoes to be a blank canvas for your weeknight dinner, ready to be stuffed and served with all your cravings.

PREPARATION TIME: **10 MINUTES** | COOKING TIME: **25 MINUTES**

SERVING SIZE: **2** | PER SERVING: **KCAL: 1,079; FAT: 90G; CARBS: 56G; PROTEIN: 27G; SUGARS: 15G; FIBRE: 22G**

Ingredients:

- 1 large sweet potato, scrubbed and halved lengthwise
- 1 tbsp. olive oil
- 250g cooked chopped spinach
- 1 green onion, chopped
- 4 tbsp. fresh cranberries, coarsely chopped
- 2 tbsp. vegan butter
- 140g chopped toasted pecans
- Salt and black pepper to taste
- 120g grated vegan cheddar cheese

Instructions:

Step 1: Preheat the air fryer to 200°C.

Step 2: Drizzle the sweet potato with olive oil and place it in the air fryer with the flesh side facing upwards. Bake for 15 to 20 minutes or until the flesh is tender.

Step 3: Take out the sweet potatoes and use a fork to loosen the flesh into a bowl without breaking the skin of the sweet potatoes.

Step 4: Add the spinach, green onion, cranberries, vegan butter, pecans, salt, and black pepper. Stuff the sweet potatoes with the filling and top with the vegan cheddar cheese.

Step 5: Return the sweet potatoes to the air fryer basket and bake for 4 to 5 minutes or until the vegan cheese melts.

Step 6: Put the sweet potatoes on plates and serve warm.

PEPPERED FRENCH FRIES

Try serving your fries with a little sprinkle of black pepper and you'd never have them with salt only again. They add a hint of flavour to whatever you enjoy them with.

PREPARATION TIME: **10 MINUTES** | COOKING TIME: **14 MINUTES**

SERVING SIZE: **2** | PER SERVING: **KCAL: 206; FAT: 14G; CARBS: 20G; PROTEIN: 2G; SUGARS: 1G; FIBRE: 14G**

Ingredients:

- 1 medium russet potato, unpeeled and scrubbed
- 2 tbsp. olive oil
- Salt and black pepper to taste

Instructions:

Step 1: Preheat the air fryer to 190°C.

Step 2: Cut the potato into 0.5-cm strips. Pat them dry with a paper towel and add them to a bowl. Add the olive oil and season with salt and black pepper. Toss well.

Step 3: Add the potato to the air fryer and fry for 12 to 14 minutes or until golden and crispy.

Step 4: Transfer the fries to a bowl, season with more salt and black pepper if needed, and serve right away.

GENERAL TSO'S CAULIFLOWER

This crunchy, delectable, spicy-sweet cauliflower is amazing! And despite being far healthier, it tastes just as fantastic as the pan-made version. Hoisin sauce, brown sugar, soy sauce, ginger, and garlic are all included in this baked General Tso's Cauliflower dish. It is wholesome, healthy, and tasty.

⏱ PREPARATION TIME: **10 MINUTES** | 🍲 COOKING TIME: **18 MINUTES**

🍽 SERVING SIZE: **2** | PER SERVING: **KCAL: 303; FAT: 12G; CARBS: 45G; PROTEIN: 6G; SUGARS: 17G; FIBRE: 4G**

Ingredients:

- 4 tbsp. plain flour
- 1 tsp. salt
- 1 tsp. baking powder
- 2 tsp. corn flour
- 4 tbsp. sparkling water
- 1 medium cauliflower head, separated into 2-cm-long florets

For sauce:

- 4 tbsp. fresh orange juice
- 2 tbsp. brown sugar
- 1 tbsp. soy sauce
- 1 tbsp. hoisin sauce
- 2 tbsp. vegetable broth
- 2 tbsp. rice vinegar
- 1 tbsp. sesame oil
- 2 tsp. corn flour
- 2 tsp. canola oil
- 3 green onions, white part minced and green part thinly sliced
- 2 to 6 dried hot chillies, chopped
- 3 garlic cloves, minced
- 1 tsp. freshly grated ginger
- ½ tsp. fresh orange zest

Instructions:

Step 1: **Preheat the air fryer to 200°C.**

For the cauliflower:

Step 2: In a bowl, mix the plain flour, salt, baking powder, and corn flour. Add the sparkling water and stir until smooth batter forms. Dip the cauliflower florets in it and let them sit on a baking sheet and set for 5 minutes.

Step 3: Grease the air fryer basket with cooking oil and place the cauliflower in it. Fry for 5 to 6 minutes per side or until golden and tender.

For the General Tso sauce:

Step 4: Meanwhile, in a bowl, mix the vegetable broth, rice vinegar, sesame oil, and corn flour.

Step 5: Heat the canola oil in a small pot and sauté the white part of the green onions, hot chillies, garlic, and ginger for 2 minutes or until fragrant. Stir in the sauce mixture and orange zest. Simmer for 2 to 4 minutes or until thickened.

Step 6: Add the ready cauliflower to a bowl, drizzle on the sauce, and toss well.

Step 7: Garnish the cauliflower with the remaining green onions and serve with cooked rice.

TAHINI BLACK BEAN FRITTERS

Every bite of these simple fritters bursts with flavours like miso paste, garlic powder, smoked paprika, and tahini. They are made with beans and mushrooms, making them nutritious. Enjoy these crunchy bean cakes on their own or sandwich them between buns. Top them with your favourite burger toppings for a mind-blowing vegan burger. You can also enjoy them with salad.

🕐 PREPARATION TIME: **10 MINUTES** | 🍲 COOKING TIME: **10 MINUTES**

🛎 SERVING SIZE: **2** | PER SERVING: **KCAL: 164; FAT: 4G; CARBS: 27G; PROTEIN: 8G; SUGARS: 3G; FIBRE: 5G**

Ingredients:

- 100g can black beans, rinsed and drained
- 1 tbsp. cremini or chestnut mushrooms, trimmed and finely chopped
- ½ small yellow onion, finely chopped
- 4 tbsp. panko breadcrumbs
- 1 tbsp. white miso
- ½ tsp. garlic powder
- ½ tsp. smoked paprika
- 1 tsp. tahini
- ½ tsp. rock salt
- 1 tbsp. finely chopped fresh dill

Instructions:

Step 1: Preheat the air fryer to 160°C.

Step 2: Combine all the ingredients in a bowl, mix well, and form two patties from the mixture. Mist them with cooking spray.

Step 3: Place the patties in the air fryer and bake for 4 to 5 minutes per side or until golden and compacted.

Step 4: Plate the bean fritters and serve with salad.

....

CORN NUTS

These salted crunchy corn kernels are addictive. You can have them as snacks or better still with a light complement like a drink, soup, or salad.

🕐 PREPARATION TIME: **5 MINUTES** | 🍲 COOKING TIME: **15 MINUTES**

🛎 SERVING SIZE: **2** | PER SERVING: **KCAL: 285; FAT: 15G; CARBS: 39G; PROTEIN: 5G; SUGARS: 0G; FIBRE: 5G**

Ingredients:

- 450g large white corn kernels
- 2 tbsp. vegetable oil
- 2 tsp. salt

Instructions:

Step 1: Preheat the air fryer to 200°C.

Step 2: In a bowl, toss the corn, oil, and salt.

Step 3: Line the air fryer basket with baking paper and spread the corn on top. Roast for 10 to 15 minutes while shaking a few times when toasting.

Step 4: Pour the corn onto a metal tray and let cool.

Step 5: Serve.

PUMPKIN SAVOURY BISCUITS

Make tons of these pumpkin biscuits as your go-to lazy side dish with soup. Or slather on some vegan butter when you intend on having a very light dinner. They are convenient and easily used anytime of the day.

⏱ PREPARATION TIME: **10 MINUTES** | 🍲 COOKING TIME: **15 MINUTES**

🍽 SERVING SIZE: **2** | PER SERVING: **KCAL: 193; FAT: 12G; CARBS: 21G; PROTEIN: 2G; SUGARS: 6G; FIBRE: 1G**

Ingredients:

- 4 tbsp. plain flour, plus more for dusting
- 1 tbsp. light brown sugar
- 1 tsp. baking powder
- ½ tsp. pumpkin spice
- ½ tsp. rock salt
- 1 tbsp. cold vegan butter, cut into cubes
- 1 tbsp. vegan buttermilk
- 4 tbsp. pure pumpkin puree
- 1 tbsp. melted vegan butter for brushing

Instructions:

Step 1: Preheat the air fryer to 160°C.

Step 2: In a large bowl, mix the flour, brown sugar, baking powder, pumpkin spice, and salt. Add the cold vegan butter and use your hands to mix until it resembles breadcrumbs. Pour in the vegan buttermilk and mix until smooth dough forms. Add the pumpkin puree and mix until smooth.

Step 3: Roll out the dough to 3-cm thickness. Using a round cookie cutter, cut out 10 to 12 rounds from the mixture. Brush their tops with vegan butter.

Step 4: Place the biscuits in the air fryer basket and bake for 15 minutes or until they are golden and the biscuits are soft within.

Step 5: Transfer the biscuits to a wire rack to cool. Serve when needed.

....

SWEET PLANTAINS

Fried sweet plantains are a sweet and delicious side that are ideal for air frying. You can have them all week paired with different foods from rice, beans, stews, to soups.

⏱ PREPARATION TIME: **10 MINUTES** | 🍲 COOKING TIME: **8 MINUTES**

🍽 SERVING SIZE: **2** | PER SERVING: **KCAL: 238; FAT: 3G; CARBS: 57G; PROTEIN: 2G; SUGARS: 27G; FIBRE: 4G**

Ingredients:

- 2 very ripe (blackened) plantains, halved lengthwise, peeled, and thinly sliced on the bias into 2 cm thick pieces
- 1 tsp. olive oil
- Rock salt to taste

Instructions:

Step 1: Preheat the air fryer to 200°C.

Step 2: In a bowl, toss the plantains, olive oil, and salt.

Step 3: Put the plantains in the air fryer in a single layer and fry for 3 to 4 minutes per side or until nicely browned and tender.

Step 4: Plate the sweet plantains and serve warm.

GARLIC FRIES

After making some fries, toss them in garlic oil for an upbeat aroma. You can sprinkle some vegan Parmesan on top for even better taste.

⏱ PREPARATION TIME: **10 MINUTES** | 🍲 COOKING TIME: **14 MINUTES**

🍽 SERVING SIZE: **2** | PER SERVING: **KCAL: 473; FAT: 5G; CARBS: 98G; PROTEIN: 12G; SUGARS: 4G; FIBRE: 12G**

Ingredients:

- 2 tsp. canola oil
- 3 garlic cloves, minced
- 3 large potatoes, scrubbed and cut into ½ cm strips
- Salt to taste
- 1 tsp. chopped fresh parsley

Instructions:

Step 1: Preheat the air fryer to 200°C.

Step 2: Heat the oil in a skillet over medium heat and sauté the garlic for 1 minute or until fragrant. Turn the heat off.

Step 3: In a bowl, toss the potatoes with 1 tsp. of the garlic oil and salt.

Step 4: Add the potatoes to the air fryer and fry for 12 to 14 minutes or until golden and crispy.

Step 5: Transfer the fries to a bowl and toss with the remaining garlic oil and salt if needed.

Step 6: Garnish with parsley and serve.

....

GREEN TOMATO STACKS

If you like red tomatoes, you'd love green tomatoes too. Since they aren't as sweet as their red counterparts, seasoning them and creating a tasty crust makes them delicious.

⏱ PREPARATION TIME: **10 MINUTES** | 🍲 COOKING TIME: **10 MINUTES**

🍽 SERVING SIZE: **2** | PER SERVING: **KCAL: 348; FAT: 17G; CARBS: 37G; PROTEIN: 14G; SUGARS: 9G; FIBRE: 4G**

Ingredients:

- 3 tbsp. fat-free mayonnaise
- 1 tbsp. fresh lime juice
- ½ tsp. fresh lime zest
- ½ tsp. dried thyme
- ½ tsp. black pepper
- 4 tbsp. plain flour
- 120 ml vegan egg, beaten
- 4 tbsp. corn flour
- ¼ tsp. salt
- 2 large green tomatoes, sliced into 8 pieces
- 4 pieces vegan bacon, warmed and halved in the middle

Instructions:

Step 1: Preheat the air fryer to 180°C.

Step 2: In a bowl, mix the mayonnaise, lime juice, lime zest, thyme, and black pepper. Set aside for serving.

Step 3: Spread the flour on a plate. Pour the vegan egg into a bowl. On another plate, mix the corn flour and salt.

Step 4: Wrap each green tomato slice with vegan bacon. Dredge the green tomatoes in flour, dip them in vegan egg, and then coat well in the corn flour.

Step 5: Coat the air fryer basket with cooking oil. Place the green tomatoes in the air fryer basket and fry for 4 to 5 minutes per side or until golden and crispy.

Step 6: Transfer the green tomatoes to a plate and serve warm with the lime herb mayonnaise.

BERRY CRISP

One of the finest baking creations is to make a fruit crisp. They're simple to make, you can use any fruit you have on hand, and when paired with a scoop of vanilla ice cream, they're the ideal way to cap a dinner.

PREPARATION TIME: **10 MINUTES** | COOKING TIME: **15 MINUTES**

SERVING SIZE: **2** | PER SERVING: **KCAL: 221; FAT: 8G; CARBS: 34G; PROTEIN: 5G; SUGARS: 14G; FIBRE: 4G**

Ingredients:

For the fruit filling:

- 1 tbsp. fresh raspberries
- 2 tbsp. fresh blueberries
- 2 tbsp. fresh blackberries
- 1 tbsp. granulated sugar
- 1 tsp. ground flaxseeds
- 1 tsp. pure vanilla extract
- A pinch of rock salt

For the topping:

- 3 tbsp. whole wheat flour
- 3 tbsp. old-fashioned rolled oats or chopped nuts, such as almonds or pecans
- 1 tbsp. granulated sugar
- A pinch of rock salt
- 1 tbsp. vegan butter, softened
- Vegan ice cream for serving

Instructions:

Step 1: Preheat the air fryer to 185°C.

Step 2: In a bowl, toss the filling's ingredients and divide them into two ramekins. Set them aside.

Step 3: In a bowl, mix the flour, oats or nuts, sugar, salt, and butter until finely crumbly. Spoon the mixture over the berries.

Step 4: Place the ramekins in the air fryer basket and bake for 15 minutes or until golden on top and the berries break and are bubbly.

Step 5: Take out the ramekins and let cool to your desire. Serve the berry crisp with vegan ice cream.

VEGAN CHOCOLATE CHIP COOKIES

Air fryer chocolate chip cookies are the best. These chocolate chip cookies have a buttery soft texture and gooey melted chips. The batter mix remains traditional but it cooks in far less time than the oven.

⏱ PREPARATION TIME: **10 MINUTES** | 🍲 COOKING TIME: **10 MINUTES**

🍽 SERVING SIZE: **2** | PER SERVING: **KCAL: 889; FAT: 32G; CARBS: 144G; PROTEIN: 8G; SUGARS: 125G; FIBRE: 4G**

Ingredients:

- 3 tbsp. vegan butter
- 120g white sugar
- 120g brown sugar
- 60 ml vegan egg, at room temperature
- 1 tsp. vanilla extract
- 4 tbsp. plain flour
- ½ tsp. baking soda
- ½ tsp. fine salt
- 4 tbsp. vegan chocolate chips, semisweet

Instructions:

Step 1: Preheat the air fryer to 170°C.

Step 2: In a bowl, cream the vegan butter and both sugars until light and creamy. Add the vegan egg and vanilla. Whisk until smooth.

Step 3: In another bowl, combine the flour, baking soda, and salt. Combine the wet and dry ingredients and whisk until smooth. Fold in the chocolate chips.

Step 4: Line the air fryer basket with baking paper. Add 1 tablespoon dollops of the dough on the baking paper with intervals between them.

Step 5: Bake for 8 to 10 minutes or until the cookies set and the chocolate melts within.

Step 6: Transfer them to a wire rack to cool and bake any remaining batter.

Step 7: Enjoy!

MINT CHOCOLATE DANISH

If you're wanting a chocolate mint treat, try this very quick dessert. These mint chocolate Danishes require only two ingredients. They are so yummy.

⏱ PREPARATION TIME: **5 MINUTES** | 🍲 COOKING TIME: **15 MINUTES**

🍽 SERVING SIZE: **2** | PER SERVING: **KCAL: 561; FAT: 40G; CARBS: 44G; PROTEIN: 7G; SUGARS: 13G; FIBRE: 6G**

Ingredients:

- 2 sheets of thawed frozen puff pastry (vegan)
- 1 block of vegan mint chocolate, cut in halves

Instructions:

Step 1: Preheat the air fryer to 200°C.

Step 2: Place one puff pastry sheet on a clean, flat surface. Place the chocolate at the centre and brush the edges with a little water. Place the other puff pastry on top and seal the edges.

Step 3: Place the pastry in the air fryer and bake for 10 to 15 minutes or until golden and crusty.

Step 4: Remove the pastry and let cool.

Step 5: After, slice the pastry and serve with vegan whipped cream.

VEGAN CHOCOLATE COURGETTE BIRTHDAY CAKE

No matter if you are a vegan or an omnivore, this cake is definitely a cause for celebration. Make two batches of the cake and ice them together for a delicious two-layered cake.

PREPARATION TIME: **15 MINUTES** | COOKING TIME: **30 MINUTES**

SERVING SIZE: **2** | PER SERVING: **KCAL: 469; FAT: 14G; CARBS: 86G; PROTEIN: 3G; SUGARS: 71G; FIBRE: 2G**

Ingredients:

- 1 tbsp. neutral oil, such as avocado or vegetable, plus more for the pan
- 4 tbsp. almond creamer or regular almond milk
- ½ tsp. pure vanilla extract
- 120g granulated sugar
- 1 tbsp. apple cider vinegar
- 4 tbsp. plain flour
- 1 tbsp. dark unsweetened cocoa powder
- ½ tsp. instant espresso powder
- ½ tsp. baking soda
- Rock salt to taste
- 4 tbsp. grated courgette

For the frosting:

- 2 tbsp. icing sugar
- 1 tbsp. vegan margarine, room temperature
- 1 tbsp. almond creamer or almond milk
- 1 tsp. dark unsweetened cocoa powder
- ½ tsp. pure vanilla extract
- Vegan sprinkles, for serving (optional)

Instructions:

For the cake:

Step 1: Preheat the air fryer to 175°C.

Step 2: In a bowl, whisk the oil, almond creamer or milk, vanilla, sugar, and vinegar until smooth.

Step 3: In another bowl, combine the flour, cocoa powder, espresso powder, baking soda, and salt. Combine the wet and dry ingredients and whisk until smooth. Fold in the courgette.

Step 4: Grease a cake pan (for the air fryer) with oil and pour in the batter. Place the pan in the air fryer basket.

Step 5: Bake for 25 to 30 minutes or until the cake sets when tested with a toothpick.

Step 6: Remove the cake pan and let the cake cool in it for 15 minutes. After, transfer the cake to a wire rack to cool completely.

For the frosting:

Step 7: Meanwhile, in a bowl, whisk the icing sugar, vegan margarine, almond creamer or almond milk, cocoa powder, and vanilla until smooth.

Step 8: Spread the frosting on the cake when the cake has cooled down and decorate with the vegan sprinkles.

Step 9: Slice and serve.

Printed in Great Britain
by Amazon

18518626R00059